But Are You Making Any

MONEY?

Stop Being Busy and Start Creating Cash

MARLEY MAJCHER

NEW YORK

BUT ARE YOU MAKING ANY MONEY?
Stop Being Busy and Start Creating Cash

BY MARLEY MAJCHER

ISBN 978-1-60037-776-1 (paperback)

Library of Congress Control Number: 2010925911

Published by:

MORGAN JAMES PUBLISHING
The Entrepreneurial Publisher
5 Penn Plaza, 23rd Floor
New York City, New York 10001
(212) 655-5470 Office
(516) 908-4496 Fax
www.MorganJamesPublishing.com

Interior Design by:
Bonnie Bushman
bbushman@bresnan.net

In an effort to support local communities, raise awareness and funds, Morgan James Publishing donates one percent of all book sales for the life of each book to Habitat for Humanity.
Get involved today, visit
www.HelpHabitatForHumanity.org.

DEDICATION

To my parents, Judy and Stan Majcher

Mom, you gave me my creativity and Dad, you gave me my mouth. I am eternally grateful to both parties in exactly equal proportions.

• • • • •

Cullen, Stanley, Coco and Marc

It's very noisy and never dull. Just the way I like it.

• • • • •

To all of the struggling entrepreneurs out there. Yes, there is hope and no, you're not stupid. Take a deep breath; I'm here to help if I can.

ACKNOWLEDGEMENTS

So many key, invaluable people to thank, it's unbelievable.

Let's start with Dr. Derek Leebaert, my amazing professor from Georgetown who literally bugged me until I started writing this book; I'm sure you didn't think it would take quite so long for me to pull it off. I cannot thank you enough for all of the encouragement, coaching and prodding. I have never seen so much red ink in the form of "feedback" in my life; I'm just glad I stuck it out. If you hate the finished project, I take full responsibility that the errors are mine and you did your best to teach the un-teachable. I am still bitter about the B+ in Business Policy however.

Ellen Pepus, my agent. Thank you for taking on this unknown ADD Party Goddess and being *so* patient. I have a sneaking suspicion that your gamble is going to be a win-win for both of us!

Wendy Hunter, how do I thank thee, let me count the ways. You were my boots on the ground, go to girl (my words), the fancy words the rest of the world is interested in are editorial collaborator. Thank you for being that collaborator and so much more to me. I can't imagine how you managed to wrangle my mess of a plan, but you did and stellarly, if I may say so myself. Cheers to many more successful projects together!

Simon T. Bailey, thanks for the fabulous foreword. I don't know who you are or where you came from but I'm glad I found you. Thanks for taking the leap of faith that together we could create magic for hungry entrepreneurs the world over.

Rick Steffann, I started this whole business thing with you. If the "student hadn't married the chef", I don't know where she'd be today. Thank you for being my biggest cheerleader when I *really* didn't know what I was doing. Your dedication to our family and the light of our lives has never gone unnoticed.

Cullen, Stanley and Coco, blame this book for the fact that Mama missed out on a few things. All I can say guys, is that I've tried and I hope you've learned from my mistakes. Coco, you and your brothers are positively deewishous!

Judy and Stan Majcher, M.D. F.A.C.P. Dad, I just couldn't write your acknowledgement without those omnipresent and vitally important letters behind your name. You two literally devoted your whole lives to Stan and me and I can't thank you enough; you pushed and pushed and never gave up. I can't even imagine how many sleepless nights you've had worrying about one crisis or another of mine and for that I'm sorry but also so appreciative that you've always been there for me. Mom, I want to take this opportunity to assure the readers that if they are offended by any of my language or snarkiness that they should blame Dad. Thank you for encouraging me to always try and do the right thing, tell the truth and be kind. I've done my best.

Stan, what can I say? Being the smart, successful sibling to the black sheep of the family has never been easy. Thank you for always being such an example for me to look up to as you raise your kids, run your business and take care of your wife.

And Marc. You're the one who gets the brunt of everything and has to pick up the pieces of my latest hair-brained idea. Thank you for always encouraging me to focus on the bottom line as well as being successful and profitable. Thank you for all of the support, love, attention, wisdom, guidance, friendship, encouragement and devotion you've shown to me. Our kids are so lucky to have you as a father. Maybe by now you'd even say that "I'm worth it." I adore you.

Foreword

WOW…WOW…what an incredible book. I kept turning page after page and not wanting to stop or be interrupted as I soaked up Marley Majcher's uncanny insight, effortless humor, and snarky sound bites that caused me to laugh out loud in agreement.

Marley's simplistic examples, step by step process, and uncompromising truth about making money as an entrepreneur were so powerful that I found myself taking a pause to reread it. Her real life boots on the ground stories made her systematic process of coding your way to cash easy to do. It was the epitome of ta-da!!! Marley has created a tool that every entrepreneur in the world needs right now.

Like a skillful surgeon, Marley slices through all of the minutiae of running a positive cash flow business. She pushed us out of the nest of financial ignorance and if her system is used, then you will find your wings on the way up. Her business acumen honed over the last twenty years has added powerful creditability to the tips, tools, and techniques that were in each chapter

If you are ready to make a brilliant shift and take your business into a new dimension then this book is your new BFF. If you are ready to take the mask off about the true profitability of your business and have a real conversation, then Marley's book is custom-made for you. If your family, employees, vendors/suppliers, and friends are priceless to you, then you owe it to them to stay out of the Betty Ford Center for Business Mistakes.

Marley, thank you for not pretending anymore about how well your business was doing. Thank you for going through all of the hell that you did to deliver the uncensored raw truth of running a profitable business that really matters. You are poised and positioned to be the new leader of entrepreneurial brilliance as the world emerges from its economic coma. We are ready to follow you and say it loud and say it proud – Cha-Ching… Cha-Ching – I am making money. Next!

Simon T. Bailey,
BizReset partner and author of Release Your Brilliance

CONTENTS

PART III: EXPENSE CODING APPLIED

PART IV: LIFE AS A SUCCESSFUL ENTREPRENEUR

INTRODUCTION

This book is for all the beaten and battered business owners out there who are just trying to make it. Just trying to get their kids raised and through college all in one piece. For those of you who have weathered the biggest economic crisis in our lifetime but still have a heartbeat. This is for all of you who have lost your house or had to default on your credit card bills. Maybe your spouse or your best friend or the other parents at your son's school look down on you and think you're an idiot, but I don't. I get it. Business is hard. Life is hard, but I can help. Why? Because I've helped myself.

Let me introduce myself by stating what I'm not. I'll feel much better getting that out of the way. I'm not an MBA, lawyer, accountant or bookkeeper. I don't know everything, profess to know everything or quite frankly care to pretend I do. I'm not perfect, polished or even particularly bright all of the time. What I am is an entrepreneur. Born and bred, seasoned and weathered, obsessed with the process, the numbers, the highs and the lows, the ditches and the dialogue. I am a business junkie. I love to read about it, think about it, talk about it.

I'm educated—I have a business degree from Georgetown—but am far from being a scholar. I always studied harder than almost everyone else in my classes and yet struggled to get Bs. I wasn't the prom queen, the star athlete, the most beautiful, most popular, or the skinniest. But I was always willing to try.

I can honestly tell you that I have worked night and day on my businesses—in event planning, restaurants, real estate, as a consultant and a coach. I have created them, worked on them, improved them and closed them. I am as in love with financial transactions and the activities of commerce as I am with my husband (and that is only a slight exaggeration). I would rather debate the topic of whether an entrepreneur is born or made than talk about clothes or politics any day of the week. I love to travel and see the world. To learn from other cultures and how they do business. I learn all day long, everywhere I am. Whether it's from the flower vendor in Bali or the real estate developer on the Upper East Side, I'm a sponge, soaking it all in.

At the end of the day I believe that business is all widgets. It's about supply and demand, passion, price and location. It's about getting along with others, then getting the sale because the client liked me more than the next guy. Whether you manufacture airplane parts or medical equipment, sell parties or pianos, at the end of the day, it's all the same. As business owners, we have the same problems the world around. They might be shrouded in different languages and customs, but the problems are the same. Somewhere along the line, we got convinced that doing business is really complicated. But it's not. There are certainly *aspects* of business that can get complicated, working relationships can get complicated, but business is not intrinsically complicated unless we choose to make it (or see it) that way.

Why am I here, at this place in my life with so much to do—children to raise and friends to hang out with—airing my dirty laundry and writing a business book I have no time to write? I'm here because I can help you. I've spent my whole life, since the age of four when I sold Shrinky Dinks door-to-door, being an entrepreneur. I didn't always know what it was called or how to spell it, but that's what I was. I've been passionate, in love, and devastated by my businesses.

Today I have a television career, tons of magazine articles, A-list celebrity clients, stars as personal friends, wonderful kids, a smart, caring and loyal husband, and the best parents a girl could have asked for. But it wasn't always that way. I made huge mistakes and I got tired of pretending. Here it is world, my own coming-out-of-the-closet party.

During the weeks when I've had some of my biggest successes (signing with my television agent), I've also had some of my most crushing blows (paying a client who owed *me* money just to get them to go away). I have cried buckets of tears at my own stupidity and the pain that I've put my family through with my pathetic financial mistakes. I've had to say to my husband that I just couldn't contribute to our expenses that month because I was bleeding red ink. Through experience, I learned that there were a lot of other people in the same boat. And this book is for you.

The catalyst for my transformation? Somewhere around 2002 I was having dinner with my parents and my relatively new husband. I was regaling them with the latest stories of my fabulous celebrity studded events, and the parties I was creating in super cool cities. My dad, a successful businessman himself, finally asked, "But are you making any money?" He thought that everything sounded like tons of fun, but was I *really* making any money? My husband, desperate for the answer to that question for quite awhile, jumped on the bandwagon. "Yeah, how much are you making anyway?" The dinner continued, we bantered back and forth, I tried to hide my shame, but that night I knew I was done. My eyes smarting as I tried to keep the tears from falling, I finally surrendered.

I'd always gotten away with not having to know that much about money because I was in a creative industry. Well, your bank doesn't care if you are creative or not. Neither does the IRS, or the mortgage lending company. Nobody cares how creative you are or how beautiful your business cards look if you can't pay the bills to support your lifestyle. I was done pretending that I had everything figured out. I was done pretending that I made lots of money. Because the truth was I didn't know whether I made lots of money or not.

I wondered why I just couldn't seem to make sense of my own business. Why couldn't I figure out this elementary stuff? It's not like I flunked out of school, or didn't do my homework. Finally, I decided to come up with my own way to understand money, figure out how much money I was making, and how to make more of it because I knew I wanted to stay in business—I could never go to work for somebody else, *that* was abundantly clear.

Ultimately, I came up with Coding Your Way to Cash—my own unique spin on job costing (a business method as old as the hills). My system turned my business and my life around. In this book, I'm going to walk you through the whole process. Take a deep breath—it's going to be all right. I promise!

So what happened after that fateful dinner? Here's how I found my way. I knew I was smart and I was sick and tired of acting like a creative dipstick—"How can I possibly worry about the numbers when I'm creative? You know how right-brained people are. I just want to do my thing!" Well, I was tired of doing my thing. I was tired of listening to myself. My stories were no longer cute or entertaining—they didn't even make sense, because I knew something was rotten somewhere in my business—I just couldn't figure out where. I was done with this M.O., ready to try something new. I decided to put on my big girl underpants and get busy.

But then I realized I had a problem. *How* to get busy? *What* to do? Little Miss Bulldozer couldn't actually *admit* that all along she hadn't known how much money she was making. What does a worn-out, strung out, in debt entrepreneur do when she's reached the end of the line? Is there a Promises of Malibu for maxed out business owners who are clueless about their costs? A Betty Ford Center for business stupidity? No business rehab available, I started by myself on the d.l.

Even though I wasn't sure how to begin, I certainly wasn't going to ask my husband. He's a CFO with an MBA and about seventeen times smarter than I am to begin with. I knew I wouldn't be able to stand one more I-told-you-so look on his face, even though he probably wouldn't have given me one. Most of his reactions to my lameness were really all in my head anyway, but at the time it didn't seem like it. It felt like he and all of his finance friends had it all covered, and I was the ding-dong batting her eyelashes at the buffet.

I went to the bookstore and bought a colorful little paperback put out by the people at *The Wall Street Journal*. They knew their stuff, right? Besides, the book stood out because it was quasi-colorful and kind of a long shape. No way in hell I was going to pick up a musty old textbook and drive the last nail into my coffin. I went through this book, full of short sentences, and colorful graphs and illustrations, trying to get back into business mode. I refreshed myself on what a P&L was and how to read a balance sheet. Oh heavens, that almost put me over the edge. But I did it. I got through that book and for an undiagnosed ADD girl like me, that was *huge*.

I went back to the bookstore and got another book and some audiotapes. I'd secretly listen to the tapes in my car every time I had to go anywhere. Five-minute drive? No problem. Time to digest a small morsel. My husband caught on to me pretty quickly—because every time we got in the car one of my tapes would still be playing in the background. He would ask what kind of garbage I was listening to now. He was actually being sweet, but I was trying to keep my audio addiction a minor secret.

I graduated to business magazines, not just the fluffy stuff, but the real deal. And more books, and CDs. After digesting so much business information I was totally bloated, but I started to get the hang of it. I remembered why I got a business degree in the first place, and how much I really did love working with the numbers. I started asking questions of other business owners. What were their profit margins? What did they charge? How did they get clients? How much did they pay their assistant and how long did it take *them* to get profitable? Were they on a cash or accrual basis? Where did they go when they needed a bookkeeper?

And then the clouds started to move in. My fellow business-owning friends weren't open about any of that information. In fact, clamshell closed is more like it. Some of them even smirked. What was with the smirk? I didn't just ask you for your social security number. They smirked as if they had the key to Pandora's Box, and wouldn't I just like to hold it in my hand.

Huh? Couldn't they just answer a couple of questions? I wasn't trying to steal their business. In fact, it was quite the opposite. It was personal; it was really all about me. I just wanted to check in. See if I was doing things right. Was I making progress? Did they have a hard time too? Any questions they had that continuously went unanswered? Did they ever have trouble making payroll? How did they know when to raise their prices? And nothing. All dark on the Western Front. My insecurities started to kick in. Maybe I wasn't asking the questions the right way? Maybe I wasn't using the right terms, you know, the lingo? Well, wait a second, I had to be using the right terms, I had them practically tattooed on the back of my hand from all of that reading and research I had done! I didn't get it. Nothing, nada. Nobody was talkin'.

Whatever, I went back to my research and started working on my own business. Not like I had a choice! I started grouping my expenses into types—a more interesting way of figuring out if you're profitable. This is when I figured out the basics of Coding Your Way to Cash. I broke the expenses of my company into four different categories and labeled them. I examined them, made a few changes, and started to have a little extra money in my bank account. I learned more—hey, if I cap the number of hours I work on this project and charge the client based on a more stringent fee structure, I make more money. I was no longer afraid to look at my monthly P&L. Heck, I actually started looking forward to seeing it!

I started applying my system of Coding Your Way to Cash to my dad's company, and then to a few projects he and I were working on together. In a short amount of time, I was applying my expense categories to real estate, party planning, medical businesses, personal stylists, graphic designers, and more. And that's when I realized I was on to something.

I was elated. I started telling my business friends about how challenged I had been and how I had turned it around. Amazing, I had figured out how to make money again. In fact, I *really* knew how to make it. I knew how to charge! Now I get it, I know why you guys didn't want to talk to me about this stuff before—you knew I wasn't in your league. No point in spending time with the new kid, right? Let her cut her teeth on her own. Didn't want to give away your secrets. Keep it close to the vest, I get it. No problem. But now I understand, I'm in the club. So back to the questions. "Do you think it's better to charge a flat fee or a percentage?" "How much time do you spend networking a month and when do you pull back and refocus?"

And then it dawned on me. The silence and the smirks weren't what I had thought at all. My business friends weren't being mean or smug or closed-minded. They just didn't know. They didn't know the answers to Chatty Kathy's questions. They didn't know whether it was better to charge a flat fee or a percentage because they had never done the analysis. They couldn't answer questions about networking because they had never tracked the time they spent cultivating potential clients, having lunch meetings—and then not getting the business.They were just like me. Good at running their businesses, servicing their clients and producing great products and services. However, they didn't know which activities were the most worthwhile or which projects earned them the most money. They didn't know whether or not to focus on the many smaller clients they were attracting or the bigger projects they really enjoyed. They only knew, just like me, that for how busy, busy, busy they were, they should have been making a lot more money. They just couldn't figure out how.

Does all this sound familiar? Do you see yourself? That's where I come in, where I can help. Let me teach you my version of job costing— coding expenses to specific revenue producing jobs. It is your road map to profitability, *the* pivotal factor that can spell the difference between success and failure for the small business owner.

By following the steps laid out in this book, you will have a clear understanding of how your business has performed in the past, a new expense coding system in place, clear goals for the future, and a plan to achieve those goals that will actually work. You will be poised to realize dramatic and exciting increases in profitability *and* in personal empowerment. You will have more money in the bank and renewed zest for your business. While everyone else in this depressed economy is trying to rise like a phoenix from the ashes, you will already be soaring! If I can do it, *believe me*, you can too.

Part I

GET YOUR BEARINGS

Chapter 1

YOU'RE BUSY AS A BEE BUT YOUR BUSINESS IS A CHALLENGED MESS

Let's start in the middle, where most of us are. Many of us wake up in the middle of our business feeling hopeless and maybe even a little bit foolish. We realize that we are far from accomplishing the goals laid out in our business plan and dreams. We began with passion and got lost along the way. What happened? When did we start working so hard? How can we be so busy but feel like we're getting nowhere?

SOUND FAMILIAR?

Meet Julia the graphic designer, owner of her own fabulous firm. Like many of us these days, she opens her eyes every morning with her stomach in knots, her heart racing and pounding (if that's even possible at the same time), and she has never looked so—what's the word? Depleted.

But it wasn't always like that. In fact, what happened to the days when she *longed* to get out of her "dead-end job" and be her own boss? She had always been amazingly creative, everyone said so. "You should go out on your own." "You're so talented." "Can you imagine how much you would make if you didn't have to give it all to your boss? Unbelievable." Julia drank the Kool-Aid, seeing a vision of herself as a skinny, tan superwoman, sipping mai tais by the pool while logging in remotely to her ever-growing bank account.

Um, yeah.

Julia did what a lot of us do. She marched into her tyrannical and stuffy boss's office and quit, starting up her own gig. Bolstered by her dreams of what her work life could look like, she did it—and only burned a couple of mini-bridges in the process.

From then on, it was Julia's world, exactly how she wanted it. Being the creative person that she is, she spent all kinds of time on the logo, the website, the business card, just the right weight of card stock for her letterhead. This was her shot. She finally had her own company and it was going to be more amazing than her wildest dreams. She knew it in her gut.

After she set up shop, home office fully outfitted, blog ready to go, special new e-mail address up and receiving, the phone started ringing. Hey, this working for herself deal wasn't so bad. Mornings, she started with rolling out of bed and booting up the system in her pj's, hot French Roast at the ready, sunlight streaming in the windows. Fantastic! Wow! She should've done it sooner!

The phone kept ringing, the jobs kept coming. So much work and nary a second to invoice all the customers. Nice problem to have! Julia was rockin'!

Not so much.

Before Julia knows it, she's on the hamster wheel. She is officially busy beyond belief. If only she could have just a few minutes to actually bill all those clients, once and for all. Yikes, she goes to use her credit card and gets the dreaded, "I'm sorry Ma'am, might you have another card on you?" Do I have another card on me? (And when did people start calling me Ma'am?) I always pay my bills on time. There must be some mistake.

Actually, there's not.

You see, Julia has found herself where so many millions of us before her have found ourselves: stuck in the middle of our business with absolutely no idea of how we got there. One minute it was French Roast on demand and sunlight streaming through the window, birds chirping, every day it's spring! The next it's a desk full of papers, far too many late nights working in a row, no one to help, a credit card that got maxed out somewhere along the way, and a mailbox full of unreturned voice mails to friends she once treasured. What happened?

Good question.

Enter the life of the entrepreneur—overworked and underpaid, bitter, broken and without hope. Mired in paperwork that never interested her in the first place and days spent on exactly what she hates most. In fact, Julia realizes that "If only I could just *design,* things would be really great." But Julia can't only "just design" anymore. She's got responsibilities. *She's got a job running a business*—which she didn't have when she was working as an underling designer for Mr. Suit.

And How's That Working for You?

Julia's dramas aside, let's talk about you for a second. How's life? What does your business day look like? Let me guess. Sort of an unplanned, tangled mess most of the time, but on some days you get a glimpse of why you started in the first place. Problem is, that glimpse is fleeting.

I don't know about you, but one day I woke up and it seemed like my whole business life was about running out of printer paper, figuring out why the Johnsons still hadn't paid their final balance (or had they?), trying to satisfy my assistant's special plan for her own schedule that had nothing to do with the hours I hired her to work, trying to determine how exactly I should price that line item on the proposal that just had to get out, um, yesterday. What happened to my dream of being a business owner who got to create and meet with clients and design fabulous parties? Unfortunately, she was long gone. Enter Bitter-with-Baggage-Party-of-One.

Let's see if you might be in the same boat. How would you answer the following questions? (Quizzes are always fun if the news is good at the end, right? Keep your fingers crossed.) Yes or No?

- During the day do you feel that you are focused on the most important, moneymaking tasks you could possibly be handling?

- Are you able to direct your attention in concentrated chunks of time to what you set out to accomplish when you get to work?

- Do you start out with a really good plan and then end up getting tossed around the ocean of life like a small, lightweight bottle in the midst of a lot of overbearing, ginormous waves?

- At the end of the day, do you feel refreshed, satisfied and accomplished with how the day went?

- Are you so on fire with how today went that you just can't wait to get up and hit it tomorrow with a vengeance?

- And then, how about life at home? Do you manage to wrap up the day when you think you will, in fact with a little time to spare, or do you feel like you are barely making it home at a decent hour, starving, annoyed and kind of raw?

- When it's time to pay the bills are you floating in money? Unable to contain your joy at stamping the envelope and cheerfully sending it on its way?

- Do you pay your bills before their due date with plenty of time to spare, or are you constantly making excuses to the phone company that clearly something went wrong with the mail because you paid that bill *weeks* ago?

In other words, if you just left the office fresh as a daisy, floating in cash with a staff that's well rested and loves you, and you're headed to the Bahamas tomorrow for two blissful, unplugged weeks of snorkeling and late night JELL-O shots, then put this book down. You're done. Call me when you want to plan a party and your budget is huge.

But for the rest of us mere mortals who haven't seen a white sandy beach in person since 1992, then . . . I think you see where I'm going with this. You're tired, frustrated, drained and confused or you wouldn't be taking time out of your already challenged day to read this.

Running a business, whether small, medium or large, is stress inducing and challenging because *you must put on your entrepreneurial hat* and delve into running the business, the mechanics of which are outside your area of expertise.

Hang on and trust me—there's a cure and it's not in a magic prescription, but in four magic letters: A, B, C and D.

Chapter 2

THE NOT-SO-IMPOSSIBLE DREAM

The unfortunate part of all of this is that you know it can be different. You have enough experience to know that other people live more calmly, at least in the magazines. It certainly seems like some of your neighbors are pretty happy, that there is something else out there. While you've got only a fleeting memory of the dream life you left your old reliable job for (and that job isn't looking so bad now—it's OK to admit it), you're sure something fabulous is still possible. And at this point, you'd settle for something adequate with regular cash coming in, but even that feels like an elusive butterfly dancing before your eyes.

SOUND FAMILIAR?

You've heard the old adage that ignorance is bliss, right? Your problem is that you're not ignorant—you can taste the possibilities. Our graphic designer, Julia, is a great example. She's frustrated and busy and has just enough time to wallow in the misfortune she secretly knows she brought upon herself. But why can't she just fix it? Going into this she had a business plan, knew what she was doing, had it all figured out. What's wrong? Where did she blow it, and now what? She's not sure how much longer she can ride this roller coaster.

YOU'VE GOT A BUSINESS PLAN, RIGHT?

We all know that long before you start a business you need to run out and get the magic business plan software that will make your future financial life sing, right? You did create that plan, right? Did your market research? Completed the fancy forecasts? Plugged in the beyond accurate needs for start-up capital and annual growth, growing at a very modest rate as opposed to one that might impress certain would-be investors?

Pull that little puppy out and dust it off a bit. How much did you actually spend in start-up costs? How did your projections match up? No doubt, you've far and away exceeded your revenue goals, and as far as cash outlay, you're way below your guestimates. Take a look at your business model. Does it make sense in today's environment? Is it a model that can last for years, if not generations?

Not quite, eh?

Negative in the Business Plan Department?

Um, yeah. Business plan? Not so much.

OK, so you don't have a business plan. Don't panic. Most of us don't have one either. Now I'm not telling you that it's not a really, really good idea to have a business plan. On the contrary, I think it's a *great* idea to have one. Why? Because creating a business plan forces you to face your demons and the underbelly of the business world. It forces you to really stop and consider how much time, energy, blood, sweat and tears you're going to have to put into your business to make it fly. It corners you into estimating your potential sales and figuring out how you will actually achieve them.

If you haven't already started your business, definitely, by all means, right now, create a business plan. Even if it's not perfect and your banker wouldn't take a second look, it's better to have one than not. End of rant.

If you're in the middle of your business, like most of us are, let's take the softer approach. Let's simply think *about what you want*.

Time To Get Specific

Whether you have a business plan or not, it is important to get specific about what you want out of this company of yours. You might think that all of us want the same things, right? Don't we all crave tons of money, the big corner office and the fancy elevator, the sweet woman named Emily (affecting a slight British accent) at the receptionist's desk fawning all over us and making sure our coffee is waiting on that highly polished mahogany desk, just the way we like it?

No. Definitely not.

In fact, I would keel over and die before I could deal with that set up. My ideal situation is the one I've got: a fabulous warehouse in a manufacturing part of Los Angeles (which my husband is scared to drive near, let alone into). The windows have old school bars across them and you enter the building through a super hip roll up door. We could be butchering meat or planning parties behind that fortress and no one would be the wiser. The floor is concrete, the wall art consists of large wooden animal heads (think bison and other scary creatures) painted to a high gloss, dripping in pearls and tiaras. I'm in heaven. Leave the mahogany and the pinstripes to the fancy boys downtown, give me the taco truck any day.

See where I am going with all of this? I'm trying to emphasize that we all want different things and you've got to be very, really, totally crystal clear about what those things are and what that life looks like. This is important. Can you please re-read that last sentence? *You have to be very, really, totally crystal clear about those things and the life that you actually want.* You can't get the corner office or the roll up door with a side of salsa unless you know exactly what it looks like.

Now that I've beaten you up a tad, let's have a little fun creating your—yes, you better believe it—vision for your future.

1. Take out several pieces of clean, white paper and get ready to dream, stream-of-conscious, freestyle.

2. At the top of the first sheet of paper, write: *What My Office Looks Like.*

3. Now, write out in as much detail as you possibly can (in fact pretend you're Picasso with a pen) what your dream office looks like. Not the office you *should* want, or that your mom would be proud of. Not the office that your partner thinks would suit you, but the office that you secretly, in your heart of hearts, crave. The place that would just make your heart sing. If you could work exactly where you wanted, out of your car or in a shoebox, in a suite at the Mondrian or in a corner at Peet's Coffee, where would it be?

   Is your office big, tiny, attached to your house, miles from home, airy and bright, dark and cozy, organized, cluttered, chock-full of inspiration or incredibly stark? Is there a waiting room? Are the files labeled and organized so you can put your hands on any insurance policy or tax return from the last ten years? Do you care whether the files are organized? Write it all down, be descriptive. When you think you're done, go back and write another page. Yes, I'm serious and no, it doesn't have to be typed (or can be, if you like keyboarding more than writing longhand!)

4. At the top of your next sheet of paper, write: *How Much Time I Work.*

5. Remember those Mad Libs you used to do as a kid? Good, because we're going to do the grown-up version here: I work _____ (number of) hours a day on the following days of the week: _____. I never work more than _____(number of) days a week or _____ (number of) hours in a day. I take _____ (number of) vacations a year for a minimum of _____ (number of) days. I travel to _____ _____ (describe the location, region, etc.—even it's just the backyard) so that I can _____ (insert action verbs—i.e., eat, write, snorkel, skydive, shop, write poetry) to my heart's content. After every vacation, I return to work feeling _____ (describe good stuff: refreshed, rejuvenated, excited, invigorated).

6. At the top of the third sheet of paper, write: *How I Spend That Time At Work.*

7. You know the drill, describe it in full detail, Mad Lib style. I spend_____(amount of time) doing _____ (type of work—designing, planning parties, writing, taking photographs). I spend _____ (amount of time) of my day working to actually improve my business. I have appointments _____ days a week. I spend _____ (number) hours per week _____ (insert –ing verbs, whatever you would need to get done to feel happier, more satisfied and fulfilled—i.e., organizing my files, following up with past customers, implementing new systems, working on incentive programs).

8. At the top of the fourth sheet of paper, write: *The Clients I Have Are.*

9. I have_____ (number of) clients at any one time. My clients are_____(individuals, corporations, non-profits) in the _____(type of) industries. I like my projects with each client to last _____ (amount of time). I like to work with people who are _____ (adjectives i.e., funny, creative, smart, dependable).

10. At the top of the fifth sheet of paper, write: *I Make This Much Money.*

11. I gross_____(dollar amount) each month. My gross profit per year is _____(dollar amount). I take home _____(dollar amount) every month. My benefits package includes _____ (health insurance, life insurance, retirement plan, don't need one because my partner provides it all).

12. At the top of the sixth sheet of paper, write: *How I Feel.*

13. At the end of each workday, my body feels _____ (adjective). Inside, I feel _____(adjective). I still have

enough time and energy to_____ (insert action verbs—i.e., go to the gym, meet friends for dinner, attend my daughter's soccer game, read that captivating novel).

Now wait a minute. What does describing my office furniture, type of filing system, clients and—craziest of all—dream income have to do with making more money and getting excited about my business? Plenty. Once you define *exactly* what you want your workspace, work life and work schedule to look like, you have begun heading down the road to success.

Over the years, I have coached and networked with all kinds of people—people who wanted to create empires to pass on to their heirs, people who wanted nothing more than to sell enough to retire and hang out on some beach sipping margaritas. Some people want a small house in the country with a wildflower garden, an organic vegetable patch, a few chickens and a laptop to answer e-mails. Others are dying for a Maserati, second home in the Bahamas, regular trips to Europe and fabulous gourmet dinners. Everyone's dreams have merit. The point is, define *your* dream, define what you want. Then you know what you're working toward.

Chapter 3
GET YOUR FINANCIAL
LONGITUDE AND LATITUDE

Yes, this book is all about how to get where you're going. But in order to ensure a more successful and profitable financial future, you must first understand your past and determine where you are today. I call this determining your financial longitude and latitude—your exact location on the map. Not where you're going, or where you hope to be, but where you are.

SOUND FAMILIAR?

So how is our graphic designer, Julia, doing? Where is she today? Well, she is frantically busy. Busy, busy, busy, earning her busy badge of honor like a Boy Scout collects patches. Always rushing around, frantic and harried, but she just can't seem to get anything done. She's behind on her deadlines, down in the trenches focusing on minutiae instead of what matters. In fact, how can she possibly go after new business or think six months ahead when she can barely handle her current client's deadlines? How is she supposed to get all of this stuff done and not end up in rehab with the rest of the burned-out entrepreneurs? She feels like she's running and running on a hamster wheel, getting a lot of exercise, certainly "doing" a lot and being "busy" (there's that word again) beyond belief, but she just can't seem to make any progress.

Shocker.

Julia is not alone (and neither are you). Unfortunately, we all spend so much time busy as bees that we completely lose track of where we were going in the first place. Trust me, it happens to all of us. One second you're white hot, the next you're drowning in debt, demoralized and totally upside down. What happened? You took your hands off the steering wheel and started, as Michael Gerber says, working *in* your business instead of *on* it. Consider this book your first step to hauling that car out of the ditch. Get it up over the embankment, back on the Yellow Brick Road, and you can start driving toward the Emerald City in no time flat.

Get Off That Hamster Wheel

While Julia is convinced she's way too busy to stop and take the time to evaluate her business, it is financial suicide for her (and all of us in similar situations) not to. We all need to surrender, to hold up the white flag and say, "I give up. I just can't do this/live like this/take it anymore. I'm done. I don't care if I have to take a job at Wal-Mart—it's got to be better than this."

The first step is actually to admit that you don't like your current circumstances and something has to change. You don't have to know *what* needs to change at this point, you just need to acknowledge that something's got to give. You're Krispy Kreme-fried and you just can't keep it all straight anymore.

Have a Meeting with Yourself

Pull up a chair at a table in the Last Chance Café. Sit down, order a glass of wine, and have a soul-searching meeting with yourself.

Ask yourself these questions: Am I willing to change my work lifestyle? Am I willing to take time to work *on* my business, every day, every week, regularly? Am I willing to rewrite my job description as the big boss?

You may think you are just too busy to carve out the time to evaluate your business, but it is shortsighted (and stupid) not to. You need to get out of the undergrowth and take the panoramic view. By regularly evaluating your company, you can determine which segments of your business are the most profitable, leading to better and more lucrative business decisions that will start putting money back in your pocket.

Today, at the Last Chance Café, let's at least take stock. Let's at least find your financial longitude and latitude. Because if you don't know the coordinates of where you are (e.g., just north of Los Angeles) how do you know how to get yourself where you want to be (e.g., on the delicious island of Manhattan)? So, in all honesty, at this moment in time, where are you exactly with your business? What is your financial picture?

Take out my favorite thing, a stack of clean white paper, and write down the answers to these scary questions:

- How much money did you gross last year?

- What was your profit?

- What was your take-home pay?

- How did that break down per month?

Where do you get this information? Ideally from your tax return, but I'm guessing that that paperwork might not exactly be at your fingertips, or if it is, it might be a tad frightening. So let's approach it another way. (By the way, if you are one of those cheerful and competent souls who has the aforementioned answers at the ready, ignore the next paragraph and pat yourself on the back.)

How have you kept track of your income? You can get the information from your business checking account or by asking your bookkeeper if you have one. Then look at the amount of money you think you spent—review checks, credit card payments, and be sure not to forget auto withdrawals. Subtract your expenses from your income, and voilá, you have your take home pay before taxes. Finally, divide take number by twelve and you've got your gross pay per month. This is a very simplistic and crude way to do this, but you've got to start somewhere.

Now, make three lists:

- Your past liabilities (the outstanding balance on your line of credit, your credit card balances, amounts that you owe vendors—including independent contractors, back rent, promissory notes, everything you can think of).

- Your upcoming obligations for approximately the next six months (payroll, your publicist who's on retainer for $2,000 a month, the property tax bill for your office that's due in two months, insurance that will be due, everything).

- Money coming in for the next six months. Forget the fancy words, just make a list of all of the income that is on its way and when it will be in your bank account. If you have an accounts receivable balance of $10,000 and your customers usually pay you by the fifth of the month, put it down. If you have a signed contract for a job and are expecting a deposit, write that down. Have a tax refund on its way? Put it down.

Now, call a friend and invite him/her to join you at the Last Chance Café. This needs to be someone who is familiar with your business, someone who will not open his big mouth, someone who will not shriek when he sees the numbers or what you owe. Someone who is trustworthy and has your best interests at heart.

Take those embarrassing lists, summon your courage, and show them to your friend. Have another glass of wine—or maybe a shot of Tequila—while he peruses them. And then, ask your friend—your smart, discreet friend—to challenge what's on your lists. He should be saying things like: "Wait, you forgot that you committed to donate to that charity." "Don't forget the balloon payment for your workers' comp policy that is due in July." If you're really lucky, your friend will remember money that's coming in that you forgot about—"What about that gig you're doing in September?" Add all your friend's comments to your lists.

Then, go back, look at them once more, and add anything you forgot. This is like wringing water out of a sponge—there's always more. But to find your position on the map, it's crucial to think of absolutely every conceivable debt and obligation, as well as every conceivable bit of income.

OK, look around. What do you see? Are you clutching bits of broken boards, floating in the ocean, the sharks circling? While this is certainly not an ideal situation, at least you know where you are. And the good news is, your lifeboat is on the way. Get ready to navigate toward your dream.

Chapter 4

Job Costing, aka Coding Your Way to Cash—Your New Life Raft

"As you climb the ladder of life, make sure that it's leaning against the right building." "Don't fill the bathtub when the plug isn't securely in the drain." "You won't hit a target that you can't see." "Measure twice, cut once." "Work smart, not hard." These annoying clichés all apply to the business world.

Sound Familiar?

When Stanley originally called Julia about designing his company's website, she interviewed him about his needs and put together a proposal based not only on those needs but also on her past experience designing websites for other clients. She estimated the amount of time she anticipated working on the project, as well as the amount of time one of her independent contractors would need to put in. Pleased with the price she was quoting (not too high, not too low), she submitted the proposal to Stanley. He signed off on her proposal, paid her a retainer and off they went into cyber-bliss, right?

Not so fast.

There's More Left in the Strainer Than You Think

If the fundamentals of a profit and loss statement (or P&L as we will refer to it from now on) are income, expenses, and net profit (or loss), and we think of income as a pitcher full of crushed tomatoes which are poured and trapped in a strainer so the juice (net profit) can filter through the strainer into a jar, then most of us have a lot more tomatoes (expenses) left in the strainer than we realize.

Huh?

Translation: *We spend a lot more time and money on our clients' projects than we think.*

Julia was so excited with the total amount she was getting to charge Stanley (that pitcher full of crushed tomatoes) that she lost sight of the fact that what *really* counts in business is the juice (net profit). At the end of the day, all that matters is *profit.* You can have all of the sales you want, millions and millions of dollars of sales, and still go bankrupt. Why? Because there are more tomatoes (expenses) left in that strainer than you think. Unless you can figure out how to squeeze a little more juice (profit) out of the strainer you could be on the fast track to disaster yourself.

Through careful analysis of the P&L, more profit can be extracted with minimal effort.

Big-Time Scary—The P&L

Remember that latitude and longitude conversation we had a little while ago? How you can't get where you want to go unless you know where you are now? Utilizing a P&L helps create the map. To many of us, nothing sounds more wicked, horrible and challenging than willingly embracing a P&L any more frequently than we absolutely have to. But by the time you're finished with this book, the P&L will be your best friend. We're going to boil it down to its key components and get rid of the unnecessary detail that won't serve our purposes here.

A typical P&L looks like this.

Sample *Job* Profit and Loss Statement (P&L):

Client/Project:	Job Code:
Wince's Birthday	12D11A

Revenue:	$ 5,000.00

Expenses:	
Food	1,500.00
Beverages	400.00
Staff Labor	1,000.00
Rentals	400.00
Signage/Printing	320.00
Shipping	80.00
Travel/Mileage	100.00
Total Expenses	(3,800.00)

Net Profit/Loss:	$ 1,200.00

The difference between total income and total expenses:
$5,000 - $3,800 = $1,200

It is comprised of revenue (the amount of money you take in), expenses (the amount of money that you spend generating that revenue), and profit (the money that's left over after all of your expenses have been paid— think of the juice you managed to squeeze out of those tomatoes in the strainer). Companies generally produce P&Ls monthly and annually.

You've probably heard rules of thumb about construction: plan to spend twice as much and have the project take twice the amount of time the contractor quotes. The same goes with travel: plan to have that vacation be a lot more than just the airfare and the hotel. Somewhere along the line the expenses for tips, scuba lessons, souvenirs and meals just seem to creep up and up and up. Why? Life. It just happens. Business is the same way, but if you anticipate that your projects will take a little longer to complete than you expect and that you'll incur just a "few" more expenses than you planned for, you'll be off and running.

These are two key points most businesspeople miss—the importance of tracking employee time (including your own) and uncovering hidden expenses for each project. And now we reach the fork in the road. *Using my system of job costing, Code Your Way to Cash, you'll discover all the time and hidden expenses associated with servicing a client or producing a product.*

To Code Your Way to Cash, you are going to have to:

1. Create a job code for every job (defined as any project with a start and an end date).

2. Organize your project expenses for each job into one of four categories—A, B, C or D.

3. Code your revenue by job.

4. Print your P&Ls by job code during and after completion of each job, for analysis.

These steps will lead you to an accurate picture of how much money you really make per job.

YOU CAN'T RUN YOUR BUSINESS BLINDFOLDED

"But wait!" you're saying, "I already have monthly P&Ls and annual P&Ls for my business and I still don't have enough money at the end of my month!"

Let's face it, most companies don't receive (or look at) these P&Ls often enough or soon enough to course correct. If you did look at your monthly P&L on a regular basis and actually pulled it apart, the expenses and income would be fresh in your mind. Clearly, errors would be more obvious because they would all be in recent memory. For example, what if your monthly P&L's expense line said: "Telephone $742," and you saw that dollar amount within a few weeks of the month closing out? You would stop and say, "Uh-uh. I don't spend that much on my phone bill!" Maybe or maybe not—that line item could have shown up for a number of reasons:

1. You really do spend that much on your phone bill when you add in your office phone, the cell phone and the roaming charges you've been incurring.

2. The P&L is combining two months' worth of phone bills.

3. Your new receptionist is homesick and has been using the company line to call her boyfriend in France.

Unless you take the time to review your P&Ls regularly and frequently, these kinds of expenses won't jump out at you and you can't correct your errors. You don't know to consider changing your calling plan or to have the receptionist reimburse you for those lengthy, flirtatious international calls.

Imagine how much more effective you could be if you looked at the P&Ls on a per job basis, once a week, for everything you've got in process. By assigning a job code to everything (all expenses, including employee time) and creating P&Ls for each project, you can course correct much, much more easily. P&Ls printed by job provide the clarity and knowledge you need to most profitably and effectively run your business.

Your New Life Raft, Comprised of the Letters A, B, C and D

Years ago when I was fighting for survival, trying to regain my self-confidence and sense of dignity, trying to convince my husband that I was not some cream puff creative type incapable of handling the numbers in my business, I set out on a path to sort everything out. My theory was that if I could sort out my business, my personal life would follow. Because let's face it, if your business doesn't have money in the bank, you don't get paid. If you don't get paid, the insurance company, the bank that owns your mortgage, the dog groomer, nobody gets paid and your life very quickly becomes a living hell. It's amazing how a negative bank balance can make you feel ugly, lame and useless faster than almost anything else I can think of.

So here's how this ADD girl did it (and how you can too!)—Code Your Way to Cash with those four magic letters I talked about earlier—A, B, C and D. They are your life raft to financial success.

How? Easy, actually.

Essentially the process that I'm going to lay out for you in great detail involves categorizing your expenses into one of four groups: A, B, C or D. The purpose of this is so that you break down each of your projects in order to assess its health and profitability. Because if each project or client generates a profit, and assuming your overhead isn't way out of whack, you're going to generate a profit in your company. A profitable company means you get paid, the insurance company, the mortgage, the dog groomer, everybody gets paid—and your partner will stop whining and you'll stop wincing. Get this part solved and you're more than halfway there.

Now I know what you're thinking, oh great, *more* work. Just what I *don't* need. Trust me, this is a different kind of work. You will actually learn to love it because examining the P&L for each project becomes a great big game. You will be looking at profitability (or lack thereof) in chunks, organized by job. My coding process allows you to hunker down and analyze which clients and projects are profitable, which are not and how you can either ditch the dogs or sniff out the profitable ones from the very beginning. We're going to rebuild your bottom line, client by client, and there are many ways to do this. The *process* is the same for everyone, but the *results* of your analysis will help you determine and customize your approach. Kind of like a tailor-made, fix-it situation for your particular circumstances. Really, it's going to get exciting because your "ta-da!" is on the way. By examining your business on a per job basis, you will understand the health of each job, and can use that information to achieve your goals.

Revenue and Expense Coding—An Ounce of Prevention is Worth Ten Pounds of Cure

Now I know that this is a major paradigm shift for most of you. You can barely get your monthly and yearly P&Ls done and now I'm asking you, in fact forcing you, to create a P&L per project in order to expense code. Have I lost my mind? Don't I know how busy you are? Didn't I listen when you said you were already overwhelmed and at your wits' end? Well yes, I did listen and just bear with me for a minute because this is going to start making a whole lot more sense. In fact, I'm going to *promise* you a great big Aha! moment very shortly.

I want you to think of job costing, or expense coding as I call it, like this: regular maintenance for your car, an annual physical for your body, or cleaning your gutters long before rain is on the horizon.

Have you ever noticed that if you don't take your car in for an oil change regularly, rotate your tires, or stop in for maintenance when that dreaded "Check Engine" light blinks, you will experience some problems? The last time I got lazy and ignored that stupid light I had a major problem with my gas gauge. Somehow in the mysterious world of cars, my gas gauge would say that I had a quarter of a tank when my tank actually was empty.

Coming home late one Christmas night from an evening of family fun, yours truly ran out of gas. Of course I blamed my husband, we had two babies in the car and kaput, that's it, we're done. Sure, we called AAA and got a can of gas, but it wasn't easy trying to scare up the lone employee blessed with working on Christmas night. My husband and I didn't speak until the next day because I was still berating him for not checking our gas status before we left the party across town. Drama, drama, drama—all of it unnecessary. If I had just paid attention to that light, my mechanic would have caught the gauge issue and my holiday would have been saved.

Not going to the dermatologist when you first notice that mole is looking a little different than it has in the past? Procrastinate a little longer and you've got a full-blown malignant melanoma on your face and even the best plastic surgeon in the world can't promise you won't have a scar.

Same thing with the gutters. We have an almost flat roof, common to our type of California architecture. Time flies and I forget to get the gutters cleaned, which seem to have filled up overnight. (Didn't I just get those things emptied?) What happens? Water starts pooling in all kinds of unfortunate places on top of the roof and, bingo, the ceilings start to leak. And once you've got a leak, forget about it, water just keeps leaking and leaking and before you know it you need new drywall, paint, have sprung a little mold, and so on. Get it? Just clean the damn gutters more frequently and you're not in crisis management mode (an unfortunate place where I've spent a lot of my life).

Expense coding is the same way. Just track and group your expenses like I'm going to show you and you'll save yourself a multitude of headaches. Some of the problems that will start to vanish:

1. You won't ever wonder again why you have so much month left at the end of your money.

2. You'll no longer struggle with pricing your product or service. By categorizing and tracking your expenses correctly you will know how much it really costs to produce that product or service and you can now rely on the historical data to tweak your pricing in the future.

3. You'll know which clients have the highest profit margins and make you the most money. As a result . . .

4. You'll finally understand why you've got to get rid of those high maintenance, annoying, nagging, it's-never-right clients, once and for all. Because they cost you too much *time*. You won't just *think*

they cost you too much time, you'll actually *know*, the numbers will be staring you right in the face.

5.   You can plan your cash flow better and not come up short because you'll know what projects you have on the books and how much money you'll be taking home at the end of each of them (instead of just hoping and guessing).

And on and on and on. The information gleaned from expense coding leads to changes that can easily increase profitability from 50–100%. The enlightenment will be insane. Promise.

Just Find the Time

Finding time to Code Your Way to Cash is essential—entrepreneurs don't have time *not* to be expense coding, as it leads to informed choices that increase profitability.

If I only had a nickel for every time I heard an entrepreneur tell me, "But I just don't have the time!" Find it. You can't afford not to. If you want to start keeping some of that cash that comes in, you've got to realign your thinking. You simply cannot afford to keep working *in* your business without working *on* it. You've got to set aside a certain amount of time each week to work *on* your business. In the best of all worlds, I want you to set aside a certain amount of time each day. Why? Because one minute of planning will save you four minutes of doing.

Don't argue with me, just handle it. Get off the phone with your friends, start answering your phone messages while you're on the treadmill, click off the remote, skip a meal, whatever you need to do to get your sweet self off your duff and in the position to turn your financial situation around. Trust me, if I can find the time to expense code—while running my companies, giving lectures about job costing, writing this book, staying happily married to my husband, hanging out with my friends and family and parenting three kids (the oldest being a teenager, the youngest in diapers at the time of this writing)—you can do it, too. Seriously. Ditch the excuses.

There's something about being proactive and taking charge of your schedule, your life and your priorities that frees you up, mentally and emotionally. Yes, I am saying emotionally, because if you're worried about money you're an emotional wreck. Am I saying that money brings happiness? No, not always, of course other things come into play. But what I am saying is that *not* having money—in both your business life and your personal life—is very stressful. I have yet to meet anyone with big money trouble managing to be very happy in the midst of it. Money trouble is so preoccupying that it leaves you no peace of mind to enjoy your family, your hobbies, your friends and your other passions—things we know lead to true happiness.

Part II
EXPENSE CODING EXPLAINED

Chapter 5

LET THE FUN BEGIN—
SETTING UP A CODING SYSTEM

If we're going to eat the elephant then it's time to pick up the fork. There's not a fabulously exciting way to start revenue and expense coding. That's of course the problem, why it's so hard to get going! You've simply got to begin. You've probably acknowledged that the picture of your business (and personal) life is a little unfortunate. Everything is in a state of slight disrepair or maybe even in shambles. How about if we do something about it? So far, we've taken your vital signs—you're too busy and your financial health is teetering on precarious, but you know what you want. Now it's time to delve into the coding process and get you on the road to recovery. A spoonful of sugar will get the medicine down! Being proactive never felt so good.

CREATING THE CODE

So how exactly does all of this work? Let me explain.

Once you've embraced the concept of coding, you need a simple mechanism to track both the revenue and expenses for each job, or project (or product). That simple mechanism is called a *job code*. A job code must be assigned to each project. The coding system needs to be:

1. Clear-cut and transparent

2. Easy to communicate

3. Simple to replicate

Why are these things important? Because not only do *you* need to understand your job code, you will need to *explain it* to many different people and organizations as your business inevitably grows. There is no point in overly complicating things! Once established, you'll communicate the code to:

- The bookkeeper

- The controller or accountant

- All employees

- Independent contractors and other virtual team members (members of your team who are not physically present in the office)

- Vendors (maybe)

So what does a job code look like? First I'll explain my system, which will work for many businesses. Based on your needs and the needs of your company, your code might look different, but the key is to be *consistent.* Take the time to really think through how you're going to set up your code because once you do, you don't want to go back and change it unless you absolutely have to.

Here is a sample job code for my event planning company: 12K01A. All our codes are composed of six characters, a combination of numbers and letters. The first two characters stand for the year. Any project that is going to take place in 2012 would start with the number "12."

The next character in the sequence is a letter that represents the month in which the project is going to happen. A = January, B = February, C = March and so on, all the way to L = December. Now, for our sample, the code for a party taking place on November 1, 2012 would start to look like this: 12K*** ("12" represents the year 2012, "K" represents the month of November).

The next two characters in the sequence are numbers representing the date that the particular event will happen. So that the length of your codes is consistent, always use a "0" if the date is a single digit. November 1, 2012 now becomes 12K01*. The "01" represents the first of November.

The last character in our sequence is an A, B, C, D, E or F. It represents which client booked us first for that date, and allows us to have multiple events on the same date. The assignation of an "A" or a "B" as the last character does not represent how much we like the client, whether his event is happening earlier in the day, or is more profitable than the other clients. It strictly represents when we booked the client, and the letters could go all the way to Z if we had that many clients on one day. Small note—we're using the letters A, B, C and D here for *job codes*. Don't confuse your job codes with grouping your expenses into the *lettered categories A, B, C and D*. If this is challenging, set up a coding system that makes sense to you

The first client booking on November 1, 2012 is coded "12K01A." If another client calls us for that date (and the more successful you become, the more often this is going to happen), no problem, we would just assign that next client the code "12K01B."

While this system works for me, something else might suit your business better. Whatever you do, remember that the code should be clear-cut and transparent, easy to communicate, and simple to replicate. The only component I strongly suggest you include is the year a project starts.

If you're a mechanic and you decide to code jobs by client name and project type, your codes might look like: 12JSMITHBRAKES (year is 2012, client is John Smith, project is fixing his brakes). If the client comes back to you later that year with a second job, its job code would be 12JSMITHAC (2012, John Smith, air conditioning). Note—if you have a more established business, you may have an accounting system that already tracks your expenses by customer order. For example, your car repair business may have accounting software that automatically tracks expenses by customer invoice. Great! Use it. But if you don't have that software, you need to make sure you are tracking revenue and expenses for every job to make sure each is profitable. Create a tracking system and do it yourself. No matter what, you need to have a good job coding system.

And voilà! You've got it! Whether you go with 12K01A or 12JSMITHBRAKES or something of your own devising, this job code is the link to financial freedom. All of the revenue and costs for a particular project will now be tagged with this code so you can see how profitable (or not) it actually is.

Alphabet Soup

Let's talk about categorizing our expenses. This is crazy important. You will want to read and re-read this part of the book until your understanding is crystal clear. We break our expenses down into four groups: As, Bs, Cs and Ds. By clearly identifying each type of expense, you will become aware of the pitfalls that ensnared you in the past. And once you're aware of the pitfalls, you will know how to avoid them.

A Is Not Just for Apple

I think of the A Costs as the obvious ones. They are the typical expenses that you would customarily mark up and then pass on to the client, and in the old days would have been the key indicator as to whether or not you were profitable.

In Julia's case, let's say she designs and delivers business cards to her client Stanley. An example of an A Cost would be the cost of printing. Printing the business cards cost Julia $200. She marks this up and charges Stanley $300 for the business cards. If she designed an entire identity system for Stanley, with postcards and a direct mail piece, and the printer charged her $1,000, she would turn around and charge Stanley $2000. In the old days, Julia would have said, "Oh great! I just made $1,000 profit." Not so fast. Julia's $1,000 profit does *not* take into consideration the time she worked on the project (her hourly rate) or any of the not-so-obvious, hidden expenses.

B IS FOR BOY AND THE BOY'S <u>TIME</u>

Here's where things start to get interesting and we begin to peel back the layers of the onion. Start understanding the B Costs and we start making real progress. The B Costs represent time—all of Julia's time spent designing the business cards, the identity system, the direct mail piece, and so on. All of Julia's time spent on the phone with Stanley, her vendors and driving to appointments. (Yes, driving to appointments!)

My litmus test about whether or not a certain chunk of your time should be allocated to a project? Here's the magic question: *Would I have spent the time if it weren't for this client or project?* If the answer is No, I would not have spent the time if it weren't for that project, then you assign the client's job code to that time.

Julia not only has to pay the printer to actually print Stanley's business cards, she also has to spend lots of *time* talking to the printer and prepping the project to go to press. In addition, she has to spend lots of *time* with Stanley to understand the project in the first place.

When Stanley first called Julia and left a message asking her to design an identity system for him, she played phone tag returning his call, finally reached him and spent thirty minutes getting the scope of the project under her belt, called a couple of her favorite printers to start collecting prices and paper samples. She talked to Stanley again, e-mailed him some mock-ups (is she going in the right direction?) and on went the cycle. All of this time back and forth, whether it's with the client or the vendor, is time spent on this particular project and therefore categorized as a B Cost.

Pop Quiz: What type of expense is on the invoice that the printer gives Julia—the cost of printing the business cards? You got it—an A Cost. What type of expense is it when Julia takes the time to read the printer's invoice? Yes indeedy, that's a B Cost. (Just kidding—my attempt at levity at this point in the process. But I think you get what I mean.)

Cs ARE NOT JUST WHAT YOU GOT IN SCHOOL

The next category? You guessed it, the C Costs. Cs are all of the little, miscellaneous expenses that you overlooked in the old days but are crucial, crucial, crucial, can I say it again, crucial, to figuring out where all of your money is going. (Hint: That extra chunk of change you just can't seem to find at the end of your month is going in two places, into the B Costs—you're spending too much time—and into the C Costs.)

Examples of C Costs? Well, if Julia wants to meet Stanley to show him some paper samples, she's going to buy him a coffee at Starbucks to butter him up while they review everything. That coffee is a C Cost. If Julia gets a parking ticket outside of Starbucks while she's meeting with Stanley—yep, that's a C Cost too.

But how do you know? Here's the litmus test again: *Would I have incurred the cost if it weren't for this client or project?* The answer is No. Julia would not have incurred the expense of the coffee or the parking ticket if it weren't for Stanley. Why? Because she wouldn't have been at Starbucks, she would have been at Seattle's Best. No really. She needed to show Stanley the paper samples, they agreed to meet at Starbucks, she bought his coffee (and hers), she got a receipt for $8 and change. That receipt is now a C Cost and would have Stanley's job code neatly printed at the top.

D IS FOR OVERHEAD

We've covered As, Bs and Cs. So what about the Ds? What are they and what do we do with them? The Ds are your overhead and we're just going to touch on them in this book. It's certainly important for you to understand what overhead is, but it is really a topic unto itself, not as closely linked to our expense coding process.

Overhead is your operating costs and fixed expenses like the rent or the mortgage, your liability insurance and employee salaries. It's also electricity, the phone bills and your Internet connection. Sometimes fixed expenses change from month to month—like your utility bills—but they are fixed in the sense that they are not really that connected to your business activity.

Now any hard core finance person is going to challenge me on this, because if Julia has a booming year in her graphic design business she's probably going to be spending more time at the office, therefore the lights will be on longer and the receptionist might accrue a little overtime. Correct, but overhead and how it relates to the process of expense coding is not that significant. Yes, the utility bill will be higher but let's call a spade a spade here. You're not in this mess because Pasadena Water and Power has a monopoly. You're in this mess, most likely, because of your A, B and C Costs. I want to put a lid on the overhead argument now.

However, one additional point about the D Costs before continuing: if you don't take the time to clearly carve out your costs into As, Bs and Cs, then it might *appear* that you have too much overhead. For now, let's stick with expense coding and worry about identifying which costs are really associated with a particular project and which need to be left as overhead. In the end, the goal of this book is to help you manage your As, Bs and Cs so that you have more than enough money to cover your Ds and earn a profit.

So, how do you define the Ds? The litmus test: The expenses that you would incur whether you had one project, one client, or a hundred projects and a thousand clients. Ds include things like:

- Rent—whether you have one client or twenty in any given month, you're going to need a roof over your head

- Utilities—electricity, gas

- Phones, faxes, cell phones, Internet access

- Taxes—payroll taxes, property taxes (if you own your building)

- Insurance—workers' comp, general liability, health

- Office supplies—reams of paper from Staples, the stapler, markers, pens (you can make a case that you are going to wear the marker out a little faster if you had a hundred clients rather than one, but ignore that for now—Sharpie bills didn't get you into this pickle, you did)

And on, and on, and on . . .

How you work your overhead into expense coding is an entire book in and of itself. For now, set the Ds aside—focus on expense coding with the As, Bs and Cs. You will certainly have plenty to keep you busy, and the work you do fixing your Bs and Cs will have a huge impact on your bottom line. In fact, I would go so far as to say that the work you do really understanding, classifying and separating your As, Bs and Cs is directly proportional to the positive results you'll experience. By the time you get the hang of it, I'll have come out with my new book all about D costs, explaining them in a way that won't have you asleep by the third page.

In the meantime, you kind of have a hall pass. Enjoy it. But if you know that your overhead is probably too high and you think there's some low-hanging fruit to pick (expenses you can easily cut), here are some simple solutions to get you started thinking in the right direction. As soon as you start even looking in the direction of these expenses, they will magically start to decrease and you will find more ways to (almost) painlessly save money.

A Few Ideas for Reducing Overhead

- Join a business network to get discounts from their preferred vendors on products and services you already buy.

- Try doing sales calls via live meetings on the Internet versus in person, cutting down on driving time as well as gas and wear and tear on the car.

- Have your office supplies delivered less frequently. Order online.

- Reconfigure the way your phone, fax and computer are set up.

- Send your mail electronically.

- Turn out the lights in offices that aren't being used. Keep your AC at 78 degrees.

- Shop around to find the cheapest fees for processing credit card transactions.

- Send an e-newsletter instead of a printed one.

- Have payroll direct deposited.

- Cut down on unnecessary printing.

- Print internal documents and drafts on paper that's already been used on one side.

- Use real plates, cups and coffee mugs so as not to go through millions of expensive disposables, which is neither good for your pocketbook nor the environment.

- Consider the option of virtual team members—folks who work out of their homes, or in states with a lower cost of living than yours so their rates will be less expensive.

- Hire an intern to pick up the slack on answering the phones and filing.

- Rent out some of your office space if you have more than you need.

There are many places to cut expenses but we're often too close to our own situations to see them. If you're going to get really serious about cutting your Ds, gather a think tank of like-minded business owners to brainstorm ways to reduce overhead and become more office efficient.

Got any other fabulous ways to cut overhead? I'd love to hear about them. Post your ideas so we can all learn by going to www. ButAreYouMakingAnyMoney.com.

Chapter 6

A Is Not Just for Apple— A Costs

In some ways this chapter is the easy part because it's really just a refresher course on what you probably already know. It's my job to simply remind you so that you can put a crisp, fresh label on it. To Code Your Way to Cash, you must organize your expenses into four different categories: As (direct costs), Bs (time), Cs (all of those annoying, miscellaneous odds and ends) and Ds (overhead). This chapter is our headfirst dive into the primary letter of our alphabet soup. Meet the As.

Sound Familiar?

When Julia first started out in business, starry-eyed and bushy-tailed, she was on fire. She had seen how much her former boss marked up basic items and thought that there was plenty of money to be made in the world of graphic design. Julia saw Mr. Suit pay the printer $500 for a box of fabulous letterhead and then turn around and charge the client $750. Wow. He barely did any work at all, in fact, it was just a reorder and he pocketed $250. What had she been missing? Quite a lot, actually.

COGS Are More than Just Wheels

The A Costs are known in the financial world as the Cost of Goods Sold (COGS) or direct costs. Cost of Goods Sold usually includes direct material and labor costs, and excludes indirect costs like advertising and R&D. These direct costs are typically marked up and passed on to the client.

Now I want to clarify something here. I teach a unique approach when it comes to Cost of Goods Sold in order to determine exactly where your money is going. A pure definition of Cost of Goods Sold would include the product—printed business cards, for example if you are a printer—as well as the staff time to package those cards and get them to market. Because we want to get a little more granular, we are taking it a bit further. We talk about Cost of Goods Sold solely in terms of the hard goods themselves (business cards), and categorize the cost of those hard goods as A Costs. We separate the time the staff spends packaging up those business cards and refer to that time as a B Cost, which will be explained in detail in the next chapter.

Remember how Julia charged Stanley $2,000 for the identity system, and made a $1,000 "profit"? Julia's "profit" is *not* her "net profit" because she's forgotten to pay herself for her time, and she hasn't considered any of the elusive, hidden expenses associated with the project. Like a phantom dancing in the night, we know we must be missing something really simple, but we just can't put our arms around it. Seatbelts on, we're moving to warp speed.

BEYOND THE As

The Party Goddess! is handling a party for ten people. The A Costs would include food, beverages and rentals. If the cost of food is $1,000 (A Cost), the client is charged $1,500 (the profit is $500). If the beverages cost me $500 (A Cost), the client is charged $600 (the profit is $100). If rentals—tables, chairs, china, crystal, cutlery, linens, etc.— cost me $500, the client is charged $600 (the profit is $100). (If you're looking for a pattern in how I've marked up the examples, don't. I'm assigning arbitrary costs and markups so you can understand the concept.)

Question: What is the profit for the entire job?

Is the answer $700? You're doing the math and thinking yes: $500 profit on food + $100 profit on beverages + $100 profit on rentals = $700 total profit.

Wrong…

The trap is that entrepreneurs often consider only the A Costs—buy a wrench at the swap meet for $10, turn around and sell it on eBay for $20 and you've just made $10. But what about the time it took to post the wrench on eBay, and package it for mailing (B Costs)? What about the padded envelope, tape and mailing label (C Costs)? Because we don't often pay ourselves an hourly rate (or anything at all when we're just starting out), we mistakenly think that the labor was free. After all, we did all of the work and we didn't have to pay an outside contractor or an assistant their hourly wage. This also happens when your brother or spouse or Mom helps out by doing things like editing your newsletter, going to the post office, and working your booth at the craft fair. Since we're not actually *paying* those people anything, we forget that their input made a huge difference, because without it we would have had to *hire* someone to handle the task.

Interns are a great example of free labor. When the economy took its big plunge, we all were flooded with requests for internships—essentially, volunteer labor. Unable to find permanent employment, college graduates needed internships to gain experience, land a stellar letter of recommendation, and make inroads into a company with maybe even a paying job at the end of the internship stint.

What we as business owners have to remember is that if that labor weren't free (because it was provided by an intern, benevolent mother-in-law, best friend), we would have to pay someone else to do it. Seems pretty obvious, but this is a common pitfall. We've got to account for the true cost of replacing that free labor if we had to. How do you do that? You track the time of your free labor on a timesheet, just like a member of your staff who was being paid, and you act as if you had to pay for that labor. For purposes of running a P&L on this particular job, you're not going to make up a labor number and write it in (your P&L will show only your *actual* costs, *not* the free labor), but you are going to make a note of it in order to account for it when pricing future projects. That time needs to be taken into consideration in the cost of doing that job. A good rule of thumb is to assume you won't have access to that free labor in the future. If you do, it's gravy.

In the end, you must price your goods and services as if you were paying for every single aspect that goes into creating them, even the unpaid labor of your perky, hardworking intern. Why? Well, one reason is that the day will come when the free labor disappears—interns get jobs, friends get angry with you, spouses put their feet down and say, "No more! I can't relax and enjoy *Mad Men* when I'm stuffing envelopes for your next fundraiser!"—and you will have to start paying your staff for those tasks, and then you will see that your pricing has been too low all along. The floral décor that cost your customer $400 six months ago now costs $550 when you really account for all of the labor involved in producing those centerpieces. Once you know the true costs of producing the centerpieces, you have to choose between underpricing the item (and making a *lot* less money, or facing your repeat customer's confusion and sticker shock.

Conclusion

The title of this chapter is *A Costs,* but what is it really about? It's about understanding what the A Costs are and how they are different from the Bs and Cs. The magic in expense coding is to learn the distinction between the As, the Bs and the Cs. Prior to this explanation and my methods, you were probably grouping all of your expenses together in one group. True, they are all expenses that need to be deducted from your income to arrive at your total profit, but the faster and more accurately you can dissect things, the sooner you can identify the source of your company's unique set of problems. You've got to understand the subtleties between types of expenses in order to experience the maximum benefit.

My key message here is that you've got to think beyond the A Costs, and capture the Bs and Cs. You already are charging the client for the As, because these are the obvious expenses. Once you've captured the Bs and Cs, you know the *true cost* of running your business, and you can charge for those expenses as well. Let's dig a little deeper.

Chapter 7
IT TOOK ME <u>HOW</u> LONG? B COSTS

When you ask somebody, "How are you?" they often answer (somehow ruefully yet proudly at the same time) "Busy!" Everybody is so busy, which is wonderful. Snarky me, though, immediately wonders, "Are you driving the Bentley that you paid for with cash?" "Do you have a beachfront home?" "Kid's college fund locked and loaded?" "Credit card balances at zero?"

What's really going on? If everyone is so busy, then why don't we have anything to show for it? Why have foreclosures and bankruptcies hit an all-time high? Why are so many of us underwater with our credit card bills, barely able to make the minimum payment, let alone make sure Junior's corner dorm is fully furnished? Well, it's not totally cut and dried, but one of my answers lies in the fact that *we're not very good at managing our time.*

TIME'S A'SLIPPIN' THROUGH YOUR FINGERS

Your time adds up in ways you don't suspect. It's kind of like a diet. You're supposed to eat 1200 calories a day, but then you take a little taste of this, and a little bite of that. Before you know it, you've consumed 1800 calories and it's not even dinnertime. Time is like that. When you really pay attention to the hours in your day and how they are actually spent, you're going to be shocked at how much time (translation, *money*) you're wasting.

Take the average client call. Before getting into the meat of the conversation, you make small talk, asking about the kids, life, and the latest reality TV show. (If you're a woman, add in a few more conversation topics. If you're a guy, delete one. From New York? Score a few points in the speed department. Born a Southerner, paste this chapter to your bedroom wall.) When you have a relationship with people, you often get caught up, and *then* get down to business. The next thing you know, you've just spent twenty-five minutes chatting and all you needed was confirmation of a shipping address, or the final guest count for an upcoming event.

My Hourly Rate—Below Minimum Wage

Like many of you, I was *busy*. All I did was work, become exhausted and then start the next day even more agitated than the last. Hopeless is the troubling word that comes to mind. Little Miss Bitter-with-Baggage-Party-of-One was expanding into a party of twelve. I was frustrated, didn't like myself very much, and felt panicked because I didn't have enough time to do anything. I literally felt like I was running in quicksand—I just couldn't make any progress.

Finally, I decided to start tracking my time in order to see where it all was going. I certainly didn't have anything to show for all of my agonizing hours at the office, so maybe writing my activities down would help.

I made myself look at the clock when I started and completed a segment of a project, and wrote down the amount of time it took and what project I was working on. If I got on the phone with my client Ned Serrio, I wrote down 9:00-9:15 a.m., Serrio call. If I was responding to an e-mail from dear Ned, I would do the same, 9:15-9:30 a.m., Serrio e-mails about venue. It was quick and dirty, but after a few days I had some data from which to work. I could actually review and tally up what I did with my time. The light began to dawn.

I decided to take things one step further and tally up my time for one entire project—a wedding—in order to see how much time it actually took to coordinate that event. I tracked my time and had my staff track theirs, including time spent responding to client e-mails, phone calls, driving—everything.

To coordinate this particular wedding, I charged the client a $5,000 flat fee, which was to include all of the planning, vendor selection, and finally my assistant and cheerful me getting the bride down the aisle on the big day. It's not like I'd never planned weddings before—I knew that they were time consuming—but until I started tracking my time, I had absolutely no idea *how* time consuming. (I should have had a shot of vodka before reviewing the results of this brilliant idea).

This was one of the first times that I'd ever really tracked my time for *everything* I did connected to a job. Every last e-mail, phone call, in-person meeting and consultation. It's painful just thinking about it. Two days before the wedding, I think I'm home free. I took in $5,000 in total revenue, paid in full, nice and early. After $2,300 in B Costs for my assistant's time over the course of those six months working with the bride, I had $2,700 left over. Magic, I made nearly three grand, bring out the Scotch! Prior to expense coding, I would have thought of that as my profit. All I had to do to get my own hourly rate was take that $2,700 and divide it by the number of hours I worked. My assistant gets $2,300 for slaving away, I show up and smashing, pocket $2,700! Not so bad!

Now remember, we are talking about the *coordination* of a wedding here, which is almost exclusively about time, or B Costs. I was not supplying the bride and groom with physical products like linens or tuxes (that is why you do not see me referencing A Costs).

Back to the story. It's two days before the wedding and all I have to do is run the rehearsal and get the bride down the aisle. But here's where the wheels came off the bus. I had another $500 of my assistant's time to take into consideration—her hours helping me run the rehearsal and the wedding. So now I was down to $2,200 of "profit," or revenue, for yours truly. But wait, there's more!

I gathered all of my own time records and looked at the number of hours I had spent over the course of the project, on site at the rehearsal dinner, and at the wedding itself—laying out those blasted place cards. Shoot me now. I had spent twenty hours working on the last two days of the event alone. I went to the walk-throughs. I took the bride's distressed phone calls, cooed as she tried on her gown and answered all of her e-mails. Then I answered my assistant's e-mails and phone calls about where the rental company should drop the tent and did the valet need a permit. I worked the event and I cleaned up. Afterwards, it was tally time.

In case you can be as dense as yours truly, let me recap it here so we can really drive in the butter knife:

The bride and groom paid me $5,000 (total revenue).

I paid my assistant $2,300 in pre-production planning time.

I paid my assistant another $500 to actually produce the event.

Amount left over? $2,200.

All I had to do was divide $2,200 by the number of hours *I* spent working on the project and I'd have my hourly rate. Sweet!

There were the twenty hours for the rehearsal dinner and the day of the wedding —running, puffing and floofing. Let's see how much pre-production time was spent. First couple of weeks, hours are logged. Got it. Next few weeks, lots of walk-throughs to check out the venue, meet with the caterer. Check. Lots of e-mails, phone calls, checking and double checking, alphabetizing. Sure. *Without* the twenty hours for rehearsal and the wedding, drumroll please . . . "Holy heaven above! I spent 212 hours dealing with that client? *Two hundred and twelve hours* doing what? What was my assistant doing all that time? What did I pay *her* for?"

Yes, ladies and gentlemen, I spent 232 hours of my life on this client (212 + 20 = 232). Two hundred and thirty-two hours for $2,200. Yep, Einstein's little sister here had the shocking, pathetic realization that she made $9.48—less than $10—an hour. Clearly, it hadn't dawned on me to do some homework before setting up my pricing module. The average wedding takes about 250 hours to plan. Of course The Party Goddess! doesn't do average—we're high-end specialists. It took me just a "tad" over 250 blasted, blood-sucking hours to get that bride an M-R-S before her name, for less than ten bucks an hour.

Now there's nothing wrong with $10 an hour, except when you think you're making *$160* an hour. You can see the problem. But the picture was worse, because I wasn't *really* making $10 an hour—taxes still had to be taken out, I hadn't figured in my overhead. My hourly rate of $10 was falling fast.

If I were a guy I would have shouted expletives and thrown something substantial. Instead I did the whole tears-with-hiccups situation. After all of my hard work, blood, sweat, tears and lost weekends, the play dates I missed with my children, the sleepless nights agonizing over the rental order, the stress, that miserable set of step-in-laws and trophy wives. At the end of it all, I was earning next to nothing. I was crushed. Crushed because I couldn't believe how naïve I'd been. Crushed because I was a smart girl with a head on my shoulders. How could I have blown it like this? How could I not have known it was going to take so long? Why didn't I just include fewer services in that flat rate? *What was I thinking?*

I was left with the sickening knowledge that I would have been better paid pulling the afternoon shift at McDonald's rather than working my own event. I think I liked it better when I was ignorant. Ignorance isn't just bliss—it's *nirvana!*

You Too Can Be a Shark

That's when the doors blew open for me. Tracked and tallied up, I finally saw how wasteful I was with my time. You can probably identify with my frustration. Now, *most* of us aren't in the habit of tracking our time. But there's one group of folks that tracks its time religiously, and we can learn boatloads from them—our friends in the legal world.

We've all heard lawyers described as "sharks," swirling around in the murky waters of life preying on innocent, unsuspecting victims as they rack up charge upon charge. Remember the first time you ever got a bill from your lawyer and your eyes almost popped out of your head? How could you have "spent" so much? How could this evil, no-good, piece of trash be charging you like this when all you did was send him an e-mail? Wait, now that you think about it, you left him a message and he left you a message. You played phone tag. *No one even talked to each other* and now you've got an $825 bill. For what? Well, you can see "for what" because it's all very clearly laid out in the bill.

I say, if you can't beat 'em, join 'em. My strategy with time is modeled after what worked so well for my boys at the law firm—track all of your time (and your staff's time) and see where it's going. Then, you can adjust in several ways. You can learn how to be more efficient, and you can raise your prices to reflect the true costs associated with a project.

By learning from the best—our good old sharky-time friends, the lawyers—my bottom line has never been plumper.

Every Minute Counts—The Timesheet

We all have the same twenty-four hours in a day. The difference between the super successful and everyone else is how we spend our time and what we focus on. From this day forward, you're going to track your time and your employees' time and your independent contractors' time. Anyone and everyone that's on the clock or on your payroll in some form or another. And you are going to call all the expenses associated with time your B Costs.

Give everyone a timesheet to complete, every single day, tracking time by job codes. You will review those timesheets daily and course correct. You will have your bookkeeper enter everyone's time into the system by job code, so these B Costs will appear on each project's P&L.

To start, what's on a timesheet? It looks like this.

Sample Time Sheet:					
Name: *Michele S.*			**Date(s):** *September 28, 2012*		
Start:	**Finish:**	**Total Time:**	**Client/Project:**	**Job Code:**	**Activity:**
8:00	8:30	30 Min	Wince's Birthday	12D11A	Reviewing proofs
8:30	9:00	30 Min	Wince's Birthday	12D11A	Following up w/ designer
9:00	10:30	90 Min	Wince's Birthday	12D11A	Inventory of favors
10:30	12:45	135 Min	MJ's Launch	12B24A	Venue research

Total Time:	285 Min
	4.75 Hours

- Name and date at the top

- Six columns, labeled:

    ◊ Starting time for each task

    ◊ Ending time for each task

    ◊ Total amount of time spent on the task

    ◊ Client or project name

    ◊ The job code

    ◊ Activity (e-mail, driving, research, whatever)

Warning: danger ahead. Yes, this will take some getting used to. Yes, you will get pushback from your staff. They will think this whole thing is a *big* waste of time and that you are off your rocker. It's not and you're not. Tracking your time is the single most effective thing you can do to turn your company around and put more money in the bank. Period.

They'll complain, you'll waffle, they'll push back and try to get you to cave and throw out this latest hair-brained idea. Don't do it. *Do not give in.* Try it for four weeks or even two. If this isn't the best tool you've gotten to demonstrate where you're wasting your time (so you can ultimately refocus on activities that make you money), then mail this book back to me and I'll give you a full refund. The catch? You've got to send me a minimum of two full weeks of your timesheets and tell me why the whole deal didn't work. End of story, track your time.

COMPENSATING THE BIG DOG

And remember, you're doing this too. Yes, you. The boss. You are also doing the menial task of filling out your timesheet. Why? Because you have to know what your hourly rate is currently (your financial longitude and latitude) in order to become more efficient and adjust your pricing. Remember my lonely $10 an hour? You might not be far behind. Hey, if you're at $15, consider yourself lucky and buy me a cocktail.

So put on your cleats and go to the track. Total the big stuff, of course—four hours designing logo—but not just the big stuff. Be sure to include how much time you spend on the phone, e-mailing, scanning, and so on. Why? Because if you weren't taking the time to do all of that busywork to keep your customer happy, someone else on your staff would have to do it. You might not be "on the clock" but that doesn't mean your time is free. If you didn't do that busywork, you would have to pay someone else to, which would of course impact your bottom line. All of this time is part of the real cost of doing business. And the better you become at tracking, evaluating and managing your time, the more profitable you will be.

Take that first step—find out your current hourly rate for several projects. Take your revenue, subtract your A Costs, subtract your staff's B Costs, and subtract your C Costs. (Yes, I know C Costs are covered in the next chapter—we're getting there, promise!). You are left with a dollar amount, which you will divide by the number of hours you worked on that project. Voilá, you have your hourly rate for that project.

Go ahead, check your math. Sigh. Groan. Moan. Yes, your rate per hour really is that low. It's OK, there's hope for the future because you are collecting information that will change the way you do business. You will be able to accurately estimate how much time a project will *really* take, because that estimate will be based on historical data. And you can adjust your rates accordingly.

CREATIVE WAYS TO CHARGE THE RIGHT PRICE

While you can simply up your rates, there are other ways to charge the right price that have to do with setting parameters in your contracts.

Anna is a stylist who charges $1,500 for her package. This includes going to the client's home to do a wardrobe audit, a personal shop where Anna finds new clothes for the client, then bringing the clothing back to the client to try on.

Anna's wardrobe audit is an hour and a half, the personal shop is two hours, and the try-on session another hour and a half. In Anna's mind, that's five hours of work for $1,500—$300 an hour. Not bad!

What is Anna forgetting? She lives in Los Angeles, and there is a huge time suck of a black hole for Angelenos. Hint—traffic. Yes, you got it, driving time. When Anna started timetracking, she realized that she was spending lots of hours in the car each day, time that she didn't figure into her pricing equation. Forty-five minutes to get to the client and forty-five minutes to get back. An hour to get to the funky vintage boutique on Melrose and an hour to return. Anna starts tracking her time, adds it up, and realizes—sob—she is making $23 an hour, because she hadn't included driving time (or time on the phone, time reading/responding to e-mails, and so on). Again, $23 an hour isn't horrible by any stretch. It's just when she thinks her rate is $300 an hour, you can see the rub.

But Anna feels she can't raise her prices in today's economy. _The good news is she doesn't have to raise her prices._ There is more than one way to skin a cat, after all. Anna has lots of choices. Keeping the price of her package at $1,500, she could:

- Stipulate that the wardrobe audit is for thirty minutes only.

- Define exactly what type of clothing she is shopping for—a work wardrobe, cruise attire, dress for the company awards gala. No scope growth!

- Specify exactly how many exchanges are included—i.e., "one shopping trip and one round of exchanges." If the client needs several rounds of choices brought to her, she can pay more for each round.

- Set driving fees based on how far away the clients are from her office, and how far away the shops are.

All of these parameters get spelled out in black and white, in Anna's proposal and contract. There will be no surprises. If a client needs something beyond what's in the $1,500 package, Anna can charge extra for that additional service. Remember my wedding fiasco? If I had had parameters in my proposal that included call-outs like "three in-person meetings," "one weekly conference call" and "eight hours on site," I would have been in a totally different position.

You, too, need parameters for your proposals and contracts. Tracking your time will reveal the parameters you need to set in order to improve your bottom line.

Chapter 8

WE SPENT <u>HOW</u> MUCH?—
C COSTS

We've now identified the first two major groups of expenses—A Costs and B Costs. The A Costs are the obvious ones that we all think about, our Cost of Goods Sold. Julia's cost for Stanley's business cards is $200. Julia charges him $300 and makes a $100 profit, right? Right, *before* we learned about B Costs—all the time Julia spent working with Stanley and her printer on getting those cards exactly right. Down, down, down goes the net profit. And guess what? Here come the C Costs, to further decimate her bottom line.

SOUND FAMILIAR?

Coco is an event planner. She is working with her lovely client (LC) to plan a spectacular awards gala for the local advertising agency. Two days before the big event, Coco is all set for a party of one hundred guests. Then, LC calls to say, "Whoops—we're actually going to have one hundred *twenty* guests at the event." Coco adjusts to accommodate LC. She orders more food, tables and chairs, centerpieces, and linens. And here's the rub—the linen company's rush charges for the additional uniquely colored tablecloths and napkins are exorbitant. Coco can't pass these costs on to LC because Coco's original contract didn't include any mention of extra charges caused by late changes to the guest list. She has to absorb this expense which affects her bottom line. At this point it seems like everything affects her bottom line. Why not throw in some rush charges for kicks?

Setting parameters to cover unexpected hidden costs is just like setting parameters to cover unexpected demands on your time. Coco will make changes in future contracts. Because she is expense coding, when she reviews the P&L for the event, she realizes what happened. Now, all of Coco's contracts include a clause so that she has the right to bill the client for extra costs incurred after the agreed-upon date for the final count.

WHERE THE MONEY WENT

I always start my seminars with a story like the one above. And the reaction from the audience is always the same. Every person is nodding and has an Aha! expression on their face. They've all been there—or somewhere similar—and can identify with Coco. They see how looking at the hidden costs of past jobs helps you make policy decisions for future projects.

Finding hidden costs, and the truths they reveal, is the second unique key to expense coding, my method of job costing (remember, tracking time was the first). When people see how much they've spent to complete a job, and ask where the money went, it can often be found in the hidden expenses they didn't think were really part of that job. These hidden costs are called C Costs, and my definition of C Costs is *extremely* broad. C Costs are those pesky little roaches we've all got but don't typically pass on to our clients—we have a hard time admitting they even entered the picture in the first place.

You have to think retrospectively, otherwise you miss a big chunk of your expenses. For example, the massage therapist doesn't factor in the cost of half a bottle of massage oil and the mileage on the car to get to the client. The consultant purchases his meals at the airport's pricey restaurants. The graphic designer is bogged down by the non-profit that wants six drafts of its annual report, each sent overnight. You get the picture. (Let me say up front that there are ways to embed these costs in the invoice so that the client doesn't feel nickeled and dimed. We will delve into this delicate balancing act later in this chapter.)

Most of us have not been taught what hidden expenses are, or how to find them. Expense coding *trains* you to track all the things you never learned to track, expense coding is your system to capture these costs. You have to make sure that *all* expenses associated with a particular job are allocated to that job, project or product—including the pesky roaches. How do you set the roach trap? You start by collecting receipts for all expenses.

You then look at the receipts and apply the simple litmus test we used when determining whether the B Costs were actually part of a particular project or just part of doing business in general. Ask yourself, if it hadn't been for that job, would I have:

- Paid for coffee?

- Accrued the train fare?

- Sent the gift?

- Used overnight air?

- Eaten the lunch?

- Driven the car?

- Ordered the hundred color copies?

- Sent the press kits?

- Paid for parking?

If the answer to the question is "no," then that item is a cost associated with that particular job. If you *have to purchase or do something* in order to do the job, that cost is inevitable and should be associated with the job and billed to the client in one way or another. (You will not necessarily put a line item on your invoice that says: "Train Fare" or "Parking Receipt." You might, however, have a line item that says "Reimbursable Expenses."

Or, you can just figure that in the course of a project you will incur a certain dollar amount (or percentage) of extra C Costs along the way and build them into the price you're ultimately charging the client.)

Code Your Way to Cash and you see reality. It gives you the facts so that you can improve your situation and your practices. Without a coding system in place, you are running your business with blinders on. You cannot continually course correct in order to increase your bottom line and actually *make more money*. It is simply not possible because you can't accurately identify the problem. Until you separate your expenses into the categories we've listed above, you can't figure out if the patient is pregnant or just fat. Expense coding is the blood test that will reveal whether your Cost of Goods Sold is just too high for you ever to make a profit with the amount you're charging, or whether your Cost of Goods Sold is correct but your team is spending way too much time servicing the client, throwing your whole profit margin off kilter.

Once you have the facts, the blinders are off and you can start solving problems and making changes at both the micro-level and the macro-level. While some changes will evolve over time as more information is collected, there is no need to wait months to implement everything all at once. You can make some changes *immediately*. The massage therapist increases fees to include the cost of the massage oil and mileage. The consultant starts grabbing lunch on his way to the airport. The graphic designer includes a clause in future contracts addressing the cost for additional proofs and last minute turn-arounds. These small adjustments pave the way for larger changes, such as setting new policies or revising your marketing plan—the possibilities for tweaking the business are almost endless. Now, you will be making good, solid, informed decisions based on reality.

In order to make these decisions, you need to have information about hidden expenses. Think of these expenses as clues, and yourself as a detective who's trying to find the clues and solve the mystery. In the beginning, you don't know exactly *what* you're looking for, but there's been a murder and the body reeks.

If there was ever a time to trust your instincts using what you have learned as a consumer and entrepreneur, it is now. If you suspect that you are leaving money on the table or working for less than you're worth, it's time to do something. You don't know what hidden expenses you're going to find, but the probability is extremely high that you're going to find something. You will uncover expenses you completely forgot. You just have to keep looking.

Two companies in the same field are both turning less than stellar profit margins, but why? The problems of a low profit margin are the same, but the reasons behind the problems may be very different. The reasons—and there can be umpteen explanations for why things are bad— may be very different *and can only be revealed through job costing.* One company's overhead might be too high. Another company's prices may be too low. Through the process of expense coding you dig to discover the real reasons behind your problems. You are not looking for broad business solutions—you are looking for the specific areas in *your* business that will make the difference between dining at the Golden Arches and a sumptuous steak dinner.

If you don't employ expense coding, your solutions will be based on assumptions. If an assumption isn't correct, it results in misdiagnosis and the wrong treatment. It's as if a doctor didn't do a chest x-ray when someone came in short of breath, then prescribed an inhaler when the patient actually had pneumonia and should have been hospitalized. *You must Code Your Way to Cash in order to accurately diagnose the problems. Good solutions can then follow.*

Focusing on a clear picture of reality—not just your perception of reality—provides accurate information that will breed positive change. The clear picture emerges from the small details, which are hugely important. Gone are the days of simply paying the bill and not really acknowledging that you spent $60 taking a referral to lunch. This shift to minutiae is hard at first—it doesn't *feel* right. However, if we're going to be in business, we have to re-pattern ourselves and track everything in total detail, at least until being a moneymaking machine is second nature. Follow this path, and eventually you can back off on some of the extreme detail work, and simply monitor the big picture changes you've implemented.

En Route

When it comes to hidden costs, there are some common pitfalls that should be avoided like the plague. Not charging for shipping charges (including delivering and errand running) is one of those recurring pitfalls. I'm not talking about postage, which is a cost most people recognize and pass on to their clients in some way, shape or form. They also usually remember to pass on next-day air charges as well, an expense that is a little heftier. However, businesspeople almost always forget to invoice for salaried employees who make hand deliveries and run errands. One of my mantras is that *staff as courier service does not equal free shipping—it's both employee time and mileage.*

For example, Coco the event planner uses a local calligrapher to address invitations. While she passes the calligrapher's fee on to her client, she forgets to charge for shipping because she "just sent someone over" to the calligrapher, first to drop off the blank invitations, and then to pick them up. But, this "free" shipping actually cost Coco two hours of her employee's salary, a percentage of the employee's taxes and benefits, and mileage on the employee's car.

Think back to the tomatoes (expenses) that are left in the strainer. In Coco's case, her free shipping is the tomatoes. If she were to invoice the client for shipping, those tomatoes would be crushed and she'd extract more juice (profit) for that job.

You can calculate your shipping charges in one of two ways. Either use an employee time/benefits plus mileage formula or call a courier service to get their quote, and then base your own shipping quote on that number. At this point you'll also determine whether you're going to put a markup on the cost.

The Smoke Starts To Clear

Is this starting to make sense? I'm not advocating giving clients ten-page proposals when a one-sheet will suffice. Nor am I suggesting you call out every last cent of postage you spent getting something from here to there. What I am stressing is that you need to understand, inside and out, what *all* of the costs of running your business are. Not estimating your costs, not being pretty sure, but knowing what your costs really, actually are. No matter how out of whack, you can't become more profitable until you get to the real root of the problem. The root of *your* problem, because each company is different.

Making Changes

Uncovering hidden costs empowers you. Not only can you improve your bottom line, you can start anticipating and preventing future problems. Based on the facts you glean from each job's P&L, you can:

- Charge clients for hidden expenses (or at the very least account for them somewhere).

- Adjust your contracts.

- Make policy changes.

- Cut costs.

- Change your marketing plan/direction/focus.

- Adjust or refine your target market.

- Use your time more efficiently.

- Walk away from jobs that take too much of your time and have low profit margins without a significant benefit.

- Offer a discount or a comp, understanding that although you lose money with these freebies, you gain something else instead (for example, PR, entrée into a client's future, or more business).

Expense coding and finding the hidden expenses have made Coco the event planner a very smart (and richer!) entrepreneur. This year, when a returning client called to rent some of Coco's furniture for a party, she knew to go back and review last year's P&L for the same job. To her horror, she found that she'd seriously under-quoted the project, so much so that *she had actually paid her client* for the privilege of doing the job! This actually happens a lot in business, we just don't realize it. She saw that last year's quote had been based on a small U-Haul truck, one employee's time for installation and strike, and hadn't included the time to get and return the truck. Having been through her expense coding training, the new quote included a larger truck, two employees, and the time to go and pick up the truck—double last year's fee. Although the client balked at first, Coco had the facts to explain the change, and the client understood. Coco got the job for a second year in a row, this time with a healthy profit margin.

Uncovering hidden expenses can lead to significant changes in the bottom line and in how you do business. Understanding these small details gives you control of your business. You *will* start making more money.

Chapter 9

But I Sell Surfboards! What If Your Business Is Product-Based?

You've been reading the book and are saying, "Yes, but I don't sell my services. I sell surfboards. How does any of this apply to me?" Just because you sell a product does *not* get you off the hook when it comes to tracking your activities. Wouldn't it be fun if it did? Sorry, no luck—you're stuck being a grownup, but that's OK. So what do you do? How do you Code Your Way to Cash when you're creating a product instead of providing a service? You switch your thinking a bit and *really* embrace the concept of tracking your time (B Costs).

Services Are for One Client, Products Are for Many

Let's get our arms around one of the most important differences between service-based and product-based business. Back to our friend, Julia. She is in a service-based business even though she sells things—printed materials and websites—*because these products are the result of her design services*. It's clear how Julia can expense code. She has A Costs—the *product* itself, business cards from the printer or the website straight from the html coder, both of which she marks up because she is not going to just pass on the printer's or web guru's wholesale pricing. She has B Costs—the *time* involved in servicing the client—the design time, meetings, e-mails back and forth. Finally, she has C Costs—those *hidden expenses,* the lattes from Starbucks, parking and FedEx charges that are needed to get those business cards or that website into the hands of the client, the sole, end-user consumer.

These are the magic words—*the sole, end-user consumer* whom Julia services. The sole, end-user consumer might be an individual or a company or a non-profit. The point is that *one* entity has requested the help, advice or the service. While this service can also include a product, like business cards or a website, *only one person or organization has contracted the delivery of a specific end result.*

By having just that one entity to which you're responsible for a project, you fit the criterion to do standard job costing. The project will eventually come to an end. A client might return later with a new project, a new set of needs, but they are different projects, each with a start and an end. Stanley calls Julia with a specific set of needs, a particular project he wants her to work on. From the first minute when the phone rings and Julia assigns a job code to the project, to the last minute when she collects final payment and closes out Stanley's folder, Julia is working on that particular project, for Stanley and only Stanley. The project has a start, it has an end, it has a name. Stanley is going to be happy or sad at the end, but eventually Julia will collect her final payment and everyone will go off into the sunset. If Stanley calls Julia again for another project, it's just that—a new project. Julia will assign a brand new job code to this new project because it will have its own set of expenses, time, blood, sweat and tears.

And on Julia goes, working project by project and happily coding for each one. She applies the lessons learned from one job to the next, becoming a savvier, more skillful, and richer entrepreneur. It's black and white expense coding because she's providing a service for one client at a time.

Which leads us to the critical question—*what do you do if you don't have just one person for whom you're creating your magic, be it a product or a service? What do you do if your product or service is marketed to many end users?* Julia creates a website and business cards for Stanley, her sole end-user consumer. You, on the other hand, make surfboards that get shipped to stores to be sold at retail, or via your own online store at Amazon.com or Etsy. Let's cut to the chase. *What do you do if you sell products?*

TIMETRACKING—YOUR NEW BEST FRIEND

You manufacture a product, whether it is bracelets out of loose beads and wire and miscellaneous trinkets, handbags, or fishing lures. How can *you* Code Your Way to Cash? Easy. Instead of measuring your time (B Costs) and the individual components that go into the final product (A Costs and C Costs) for that one consumer who signed on the dotted line (what the folks who sell services are doing), *you measure your time (B costs) in connection with your activities to sell or produce a given line of product and/or services. In this case, you will be producing a P&L for each of your "lines of business."*

As the manufacturer of products for several, or even a large number of end-users, you can't possibly track your time and materials in the standard job costing system for each individual item you make or sell. You need another way. You are still going to be a track-master, but you become the track-master of *time as it relates to certain activities,* as opposed to specific customers. That time being your time and your staff's time—your assistant, salesperson (or people), publicist and all of the other ancillary bodies out there who are making, pitching, selling or shipping that product.

Note—if you are a shopkeeper who sells the same products year after year, you would use the same thought process and track your time as it relates to certain activities (as opposed to specific customers), just like our manufacturer would above.

DOING OR ACCOMPLISHING?

As the big boss, it's so easy to trick yourself into thinking that you work all the time. We're all *so* busy. In fact, we've never been busier. Busy doing, doing, doing. But what are we so busy actually *accomplishing?* Somewhere along the line it became a badge of honor to swirl in circles creating lots of mostly needless motion, while losing sight of what we're actually trying to accomplish. We lose sight of our goals. We need to be constantly asking ourselves, "What's the point?" What's the point of making all of those sales calls, sending out all of these samples, or spending endless hours at the Chamber of Commerce functions? What, specifically, in terms of real dollars and cents, are you getting out of all of this busy-ness?

Swat that busy bee out of your life once and for all. Who cares how busy you are anyway? Seriously, no one cares. They might care for a second, but then they're on to their own soap opera. Put down your cross, the martyr thing gets old. But you do need to know which of your activities are most beneficial to your company, and the only way to answer that question is to track your time. Did anything profitable result from that expensive networking lunch (complete with meal, tip to the valet, mileage on your car, and two hours of your time, gone)? By assessing how time is spent, you can increase profitability by focusing on your most beneficial activities.

HOW TO ORGANIZE—THE CLOCK IS TICKING

Let's get out of the clouds now and be practical. What do I mean when I say that you've got to track your time by activity? How does that relate to your down-to-earth existence of phone calls, e-mails and attending Rotary lunches? First, you make a list of your major activities, then you assign a code to each. (As with expense coding for service-related businesses, I recommend you include the year in your coding system. For example, "12" for the year 2012.)

Let's take some of the common time suckers, er, *ways* to spend our days and create a sample list of typical activities and codes:

- Phone calls and e-mails to past and potential clients—12Sales

- E-mails and calls pitching your company to the local media, including interviews—12Media

- Sending out samples—12Sample

- Blogging—12Blog

- Networking—12Networking

And so on . . . List all of the activities that take up so much of our time and cause the crazy games to begin. Now there is one caveat here. Don't go code crazy and go from zero codes to millions. Create codes for the most important activities that make sense for your business. You don't want only two codes, but no need to overdo it. If you want to include all of your sales, marketing and networking as one code because that makes sense to you, then you could get rid of the 12Networking code and put everything in 12Sales. Likewise, if you spend a lot of time blogging and want to know if it's worth it, you might have a 12Blog code. However, if you think it makes more sense to load all of your (and your staff's) social media activity into one code, you can do that. Get only as granular as will help you run your business. Codes for codes' sake alone don't help.

Next, create a timesheet, to be filled out daily by you and everyone else in your company, similar to the one we described in Chapter 7, with only slightly different categories:

- Name and date at the top

- Five columns, labeled:

    ◊ Starting time for each task

    ◊ Ending time for each task

    ◊ Total amount of time spent on the task

    ◊ The activity code

    ◊ Specifics about the activity (samples sent to *Men's Fitness*)

Sample Activities Time Sheet:				
Name: *Michele S.*			**Date(s):** *September 29, 2012*	
Start:	**Finish:**	**Total Time:**	**Activity Code:**	**Specifics:**
8:00	8:30	30 Min	12Sample	Sent samples to Men's Fitness
8:30	9:00	30 Min	12Social Media	Blogging
Total Time:		60 Min		
		1 Hours		

If you do decide to take my suggestion and lump similar activities like social media, into one code (12Social Media), then for the last column (Specifics about the activity) you could enter "Blogging" (as opposed to having a specific code for blogging—12Blog—and entering something as specific as "color trends for the fall season" in that last column).

The codes from the timesheets will be entered into the computer and the P&Ls will now show how much time is spent within different activity categories. Remember that many accounting systems enable you to enter timesheets and generate job tracking. Others don't, and so it will need to be done in a spreadsheet like Excel.

As with time, any expenses associated with a particular activity will also be tagged with that code. If you attend a conference to drum up new business, your travel expenses would be tagged "12Networking." And yes, I see the questions coming: What if I have three conferences this year, all for the purpose of networking? How will I know which conference is bringing in the business, if they are all tagged "12Networking"? The answer is in your support documents, your back-up, easily obtained from your bookkeeper. Your back-up contains all the specifics about employee time and costs associated with a particular line item on the P&L. You could figure out why staff wages totaled $2,452 on March's P&L by consulting your back-up—you'd see the list of everything that comprised that figure. And you would know how much that networking trip to the Cayman Islands cost because in the back-up documents you would see the entry for "Cayman Islands Conference and Tours, $5,000."

Review your job P&Ls (and back-up documents if necessary) weekly, looking for totals and patterns. Now you might think that this isn't practical, but remember, you are not going to have to review job P&Ls with back-up for the rest of your life, just while you get acclimated. If you let this go longer than weekly, it will be too overwhelming to catch up. Ask questions. How much time do your people spend following up with new clients? None? Then maybe that's why sales are down this year. How much time is spent pitching the media? Lots? Then you better have the cover of *Time* magazine to show for it. And, if you are getting lots of media coverage, have you actually noticed a bump in sales?

From the information you glean, you can adjust where you (and your staff) put your time.

What's Your Time Worth?

How do you know if all of that time spent shipping, calling and e-mailing samples is worth it? Well, after tracking your time and expenses using the code, you see how much business comes out of that particular *activity*. How do you do this? You look for results that you can tag to expenses on your P&L. For example, let's say that the staff spent a week sending out sales letters and postcards and following up with past clients. In your business, your lead time is pretty short. With effort like that, the phone should start ringing in a week or so. Let's say that it's been three weeks and barely a blip on the radar screen. Not much new activity seems to have been generated. The bottom line? The results of your big sales push didn't materialize. There could be lots of reasons for this. Maybe your postcard got lost in everyone's junk mail. Maybe the copy didn't catch your customers' attention. But by reviewing your P&Ls weekly, you'll be engaged and paying attention so you can course correct. Either revise the postcard or try a different medium to get your message across.

Here's another example. Say there's a two-month period in which you ratchet things up, sending out samples of your cologne. But now you're working smart and you set up a code for this activity—12Sample. You're tracking your time and costs, so you know the cost of sending these samples is $5,000 (time, product and FedEx fees). You send out samples to the press, bloggers, storeowners, anyone you can think of. Wonder of wonders, you end up with a huge chunk of business because the writer at *Men's Fitness* loved the sample you sent, and wrote a story that directly resulted in your product being picked up by Neiman Marcus. $5,000 brought you a $100,000 order. Fantastic!

But what if the results of your tracking aren't so rosy? What if you attend networking meetings night after night, miss your daughter's school play, parent/teacher conference, and your wife's birthday and you've got nothing to show for it? Believe me, I've been there. Because you're tracking your time, you're creating your own scorecard.   Well,   now you *know* that you can definitely give up the membership to the Surfboard Society of America because for the last year you've spent countless hours donating your time, resources and time (I want to say that again) and you've gotten absolutely nothing out of it besides a muffin top and a few unnecessary headaches associated with jug wine and bad hors d'oeuvres. By giving up that time suck, you have the time and energy to put into more beneficial activities. Just like the service providers, you Code Your Way to Cash and tweak your actions along the way.

NETWORKING

I bring up networking as its own activity category because, at this point in my career, networking is one of the single most important things I can do as I suspect it is for many entrepreneurs. In fact, for me, the top three activities that bring in money and expand my career are networking (with current, future/hopeful, and past clients), speaking, and designing/ dreaming/envisioning new ideas for my brand and projects. How do I know that those three activities are the absolute best way that I can spend my time? Because I've tracked my time *and* the results. And I haven't just tracked the results for a week or so—I continuously track them and let those results be the compass by which I decide how to spend my time.

Networking encompasses all of the time you spend sweet-talking, golfing, lunching, having coffee, hanging out at cocktail parties, schmoozing—whatever you want to call it—in search of new business or to maintain relationships. There's a fabulous author of whom I am tremendously enamored, Harvey Mackay, who wrote a great book called *The Harvey Mackay Rolodex Network Builder.* Mackay essentially says that your network is your net worth. He's right! Let's face it, if you're one of the last two candidates for a project and the boss's wife is your bff, guess what? That relationship will probably tip you over into being the last man standing. Networking is vital to our businesses, our lives, our children's lives, no question. But here's the snag. You've got to know (by tracking) the *results* of your networking, so you can choose where best to put your networking time.

For example, I know for a fact that if I head down to the Cayman Islands for a particular wedding planner's conference, I am going to get new clients for my coaching business. It's a given. Do I fly down there, credit card machine in hand, ready to take orders? Not exactly. But I do carve out the time in my schedule (and save up the money ahead of time and make sure it's in the marketing budget) to make a pit stop for a little face time with my target audience. I *know* that being there will be beneficial for my business. Why? Because I've done my homework. I know the demographics of the attendees and speakers.

I take that time out of my schedule for a number of reasons. I love the Caribbean. Yes, it's selfish of me. I love the beautiful turquoise water, the night snorkeling, the frothy piña coladas. When I am in that environment, I clear my head, hit reset, mellow out and create opportunities. Plus, I want to hear what all the other wedding planners are up to in their markets—what trends they see happening, what's keeping them up at night, what's really bugging them about their businesses and holding them back from landing the next big client or hitting the six-figure mark with their events. I listen, pay attention, ask questions and learn. I sincerely want to know what's up. And as a result, I get coaching business.

How? Well, there's the give and take of the conversations. All the while I'm asking questions and learning about them, they are also asking about me. Yes, I share. I currently plan events and I love it, but another passion of mine is helping entrepreneurs succeed, thrive and do what makes their hearts sing as much of the time as possible. The other planners become intrigued, ask more questions, and sometimes (if the planets are aligned) make a connection with me and decide that I just might be the one to scratch that itch in their business that they haven't been able to reach. Is this calculated on my part? Am I jetting off to a faraway paradise to prey on unsuspecting wedding planners raw with emotion? Of course not. It just happens. The moral of the story? Networking is absolutely a worthwhile way for me to spend my time. I know this, because I've got the data.

I assigned a code to the activity of networking, 12Networking (all of the time that I spend networking in the year 2012 gets this code). For the Cayman Islands wedding planner conference, I assign all of my trip expenses to 12Networking—the flight, hotel, time away, tips, cocktails, conference fee and whatever other costs are involved. Let's say the trip costs me $5,000. I know that I need to generate $5,000 in business profit after costs *at least* for me to justify the trip. Note that I did *not* say $5,000 in business. I mean $5,000 net profit, after all material and labor costs and expenses, including the costs associated with obtaining that particular customer. That's a pretty big number for a small business to swallow. But if my expenses for that trip are $5,000 and I end up selling $20,000 of coaching as a result, do you think my trip was worthwhile? Let's see, sell $20,000, subtract $5,000 to go to the conference, $15,000 net profit—sounds pretty good to me. My networking time had a very good return on investment when you consider that I was gone for three days and netted $15,000—I was effectively paid $5,000 a day. I'm slightly oversimplifying, but you get the point.

ENLIGHTENMENT

When you spend some time tracking your activities in detail, your life becomes more streamlined and focused. You can let go of some things because you know where it's best to put your time. You can determine whether or not you get a return on your investment of time by sending out those samples, or showing up at all of those industry cocktail hours. You know, *exactly,* in dollars and cents, what you got out of any particular activity. And you know which activities to cut out and which to expand upon.

In other words, see you in the Cayman Islands, baby, because *tracking your time is worth it.*

Part III
EXPENSE CODING APPLIED

Chapter 10

Just Do It—Start To Code Your Way to Cash

You wouldn't set out to renovate your kitchen without a plan. You would think about where the refrigerator should go in relation to the oven and sink, and where the dishes and food should be stored. The planning stage is not fun, but it is the necessary groundwork that will affect everything you cook (and clean) once the kitchen is complete. You wouldn't do it with your kitchen, you shouldn't do it with expense coding. You've got to get your system up and running. There are decisions that should be well thought out from the get-go or you'll regret it big time.

Time To Dig In

Now it's time for you to *practice* some expense coding. We've covered the basics—how we categorize our expenses into As, Bs, Cs and Ds. Practice makes perfect—let's begin. Many accounting systems enable you to enter timesheets and generate job tracking data. Others don't, so it needs to be done manually or in a spreadsheet like Excel. Either way, the following section describes how to physically code your costs and produce project P&Ls.

So what do you need to get this process going? Not much. Later we'll upgrade the system but for now I want you to have:

- A big stack of white paper (I actually like using the 11" x 17" ledger paper that accountants use, found at your local office supply store, so I can have a little extra space)

- Several pencils with new erasers or eraser tops

- A big pink eraser for bigger messes

- An electric pencil sharpener right next to you

- A calculator that's big, simple and easy to use

- Your computer with Excel software loaded on it if you absolutely must get fancy, are very smart, have lots of data to enter, and already have an idea about how we're doing all of this. (Giant note: do not let the computer get in your way, at this point we're practicing. Old-fashioned pencil and paper will work just fine.)

- A box of Kleenex

Set aside two hours a day, for several days. Why just two hours at a time? Because when you're new at expense coding, it might seem overwhelming. Remember, we're in a marathon, not a sprint. I'd rather have you stop *before* you get bitter and hungry than work an extra half an hour and say that expense coding is just too much and give up. Focus in small chunks, master a nugget, take a break and come back to it the next day.

When you begin coding regularly, I strongly suggest you look at your calendar and schedule these chunks of time for the whole week. It's like Stephen Covey says—if you don't put the big rocks in the jar first they won't fit in later when the little rocks are taking up all the space. Plan these chunks of time in your calendar, and do your expense coding in an environment where you're not distracted or tempted to quit. Schedule all of your other miscellaneous garbage—like e-mails, phone calls, and so on—after you've completed your expense coding. Better yet, after you've worked your two-hour chunk, take a walk around the block or a little break and then go back to the drivel that takes up so much of our time.

A CASE STUDY—JULIA

For this initial exercise, Julia selects the project she did for her client Stanley—designing and printing his letterhead, business cards and envelopes. In addition, she created a website for Stanley (outsourcing the html coding to an independent contractor who works on her virtual team).

Julia needs to collect all the expenses associated with Stanley's project, so she pulls the invoices from her printing vendor, her virtual computer associate, as well as the UPS bill she incurred for sending off the box of business cards when they came in. Wait, she took Stanley out to lunch when they were deciding on paper samples for the business cards. Should she include that receipt in this batch? Can't hurt, it was related to this project after all.

Oops, and then there was the credit card charge to GoDaddy.com for reserving the domain name. Let's add that in too. See where I'm going with this?

DECONSTRUCTING THE POT OF SOUP

All of the receipts now in a pile staring her down, clean white paper, pencil and calculator at the ready, it's time for Julia to examine each receipt and list the amount that relates to this project on a clean piece of paper. Now what do I mean when I say to write down the amount *that relates to this project?* I say this because the invoice from Julia's virtual computer associate might contain charges for other projects Julia's got going. Because we're only analyzing one project at a time, Julia is going to ignore the expenses related to the other project and list only the total number of hours or expenses that relate to Stanley's. (If you want to go the OCD route, by all means take the particular invoice and assign codes to Stanley's job and the other projects that are also on that invoice. I'm fine, though, if you just label Stanley's at this point, because we're just *practicing.* If we weren't practicing, you'd have to label the invoice with all of the different projects.) After Julia has written the expenses down on her clean, white piece paper, she tallies them up. This total represents the expenses for the project. Simple enough? Now it's your turn.

A Case Study—Yourself

Time to get your hands dirty! Pull out one of your past projects to use as a test case for practicing and learning how to expense code. Gather all of the receipts and vendor invoices, timesheets, anything that happened to relate to the expenses of working on the particular project you're using as your case study.

Now that you've pulled all the paperwork you think you need, go back one more time. Review your checking account for cleared checks and debits, pull your credit card statements and scan them—searching for clues about any expenses you might have forgotten. Careful though! You don't want to double count expenses by coding both the vendor invoice and the check or credit card charge used to pay for them.

Once you've collected all of these annoying pieces of paper, photocopy everything and use the copies for the task ahead. (This way, if an invoice details expenses for more than one project, you can just cross those expenses off the photocopy without damaging the original document.) Finally, get a big Ziploc bag, sealable plastic envelope, or something that will keep them all together so you won't have to repeat the search.

Now it's time to start implementing what you've learned about expense coding.

- Take your clean, white paper. Label one sheet "A Costs," one "B Costs," and one "C Costs."

- Yes, you guessed it. Take the photocopies of all those scraps of paper related to your project—receipts and vendor invoices, timesheets, credit card bills, bank statements—and transfer the numbers to the appropriate list of expenses. For each expense, ask yourself, is this an A, B or C Cost? Remember, the Cost of Goods Sold is A Costs, time is B Costs, and hidden costs are C Costs. (With regards to photocopying, yes, it is extra work. However, I like to have the separate documentation—it makes it easier for me. Once you understand the process and are comfortable with it, you don't have to photocopy everything. Later it will become your choice. For now, stick with my plan.)

- Be sure to list *all of your and everyone else's time* on the B sheet. Not sure exactly how much time you spent working on the project? For now, guess. Guessing at this point is better than nothing. (Going forward, you'll be recording your time on a timesheet, just like lawyers do!)

- Spend a lot of time on the Cs. This is crucial. Brainstorm and list every single expense you can think of. Remember the litmus test: *If I hadn't had that particular client/job/project, would I have incurred the expense?* If I hadn't had Betsy as a client, would I have gotten that parking ticket at the flower market? If the answer is "No, I wouldn't have incurred that expense if it weren't for Betsy because I wouldn't have been at the flower market at all," then you count the expense of the parking ticket as a C Cost for that project. Sit for a while, mull, ponder, dig deep to create this list. I guarantee you'll have a bunch of "Oh, yeahs!" (As in "Oh, yeah, I forgot about that expense!")

- At the bottom of each of your sheets (A, B and C), total all of the expenses.

- Take a final, fourth sheet of paper. Label it "Project Summary." At the top, list the revenue from the job (the total amount of money you collected from the client, excluding tips and sales tax). Now, subtract the totals from your A, B and C sheets from your revenue. The number you see is your bottom line, or gross profit, for that project.

It's OK if you're crying after seeing the bottom line—we've all been there. In fact, if you're not crying, you probably forgot about some expenses. Now that I think about it, I don't think I've ever coached anyone who wasn't feeling pretty hopeless at seeing their own bottom line. Grab those tissues, get it out of your system, and let's move on to more practice.

Practice, practice, practice. Do at least two more case studies on yourself, using completed projects. Are you feeling the pain? Good, you've done it right—no pain, no gain. Let's toss around what you've learned.

Can you see that *there are more tomatoes in the strainer than you think?* Where is your money going? Aha! You can now see it disappearing through all those different crevices. The Aha! moments continue, and you get a thrill because you're starting to see where the money is disappearing. This thrill is the candy that motivates you. There's a new way to do business and you can make more money if you put it into practice. Once you see what you can do differently, you can take that knowledge, learn from your mistakes, and course correct.

The Point—The Benefits of Job Costing

So, why should you spend all of this time sorting through this alphabet soup? So many reasons—let me count the ways! At the end of the day, job costing helps you to figure out exactly which areas of your business are profitable and which aren't. You can identify the trouble spots so you can actually fix them, instead of thinking that your whole company is in trouble. That's actually one of the reasons I came up with this process—to be able to pinpoint the areas of my business that *weren't* causing me trouble. I wanted to find the weak spots where money was leaking out of my bank account and leave the parts of my business that were profitable alone. Later, I would go back to the parts that were profitable and actually expand those areas. No throwing out the baby with the bathwater! Make sense?

Through expense coding, you can:

1. Determine the profit or loss for each job and calculate the profit percentage of each job.

2. Sort each job by gross sales and total profit to determine whether or not the highest grossing jobs actually make the most money.

3. Evaluate the profitability of each line item in order to determine which areas of the business make (or lose) the most money.

4. Determine which segments of the business to grow, and which to eliminate. (For example, Julia now knows that she can double her printer's charge for business cards, an A Cost, when she invoices the end user with very little additional labor, a B Cost. She also sees that creating websites has a relatively low profit margin, considering her A and B Costs. She can stop focusing on websites and turn her attention to getting more clients who want business cards.)

When you Code Your Way to Cash, you can stop spinning your wheels once and for all and focus on what aspects of your business really need your attention. Hamsters, it's time to get off the wheel; you have now graduated to the Habitrail.

A Place for Everything—Setting Up Your Filing System

Before you can implement your new system, you have to have a place to put things. You need to reorganize your filing system. Make it easy on yourself, don't worry about your old jobs. Start fresh, looking forward.

1. First, pick a folder color for all *vendor files*. You will have two groups of vendor folders, both the same color:

   a. Folders for vendors you use all the time. Each of these files will be labeled with the year and the vendor name. For example, "12 Apple" to "12 Zebra's Camera Shop."

   b. Twenty-six folders for all your one-off vendors, vendors you don't use enough to warrant having their own folders. Label these "12 Miscellaneous A" to "12 Miscellaneous Z." 12 Miscellaneous A will hold miscellaneous vendor folders for the year 2012 whose names (company names or individual names) start with the letter "A."

   c. File your vendor folders alphabetically.

   d. Special note: What time of year are you doing this? If you're reorganizing in March, of course create new vendor folders. If you're reorganizing in November, create new vendor folders for the next year.

2. Second, pick another color folder for all client files (unless you're the type that prefers binders because of the size of your projects—use whatever works best for you and your type of business). Label these with the client name, the name of project, and the job code. For example, "Majcher, Marley, Giant Party, 12K01A." If you want to get really compulsive, you can physically write the date on the folder as well. I actually find this makes things easier: "Majcher, Marley, Giant Party, November 1, 2012, 12K01A." I file my client folders by job code because that's what makes the most sense for my company. If you want to file yours alphabetically by project, that's fine. The key is to be consistent.

3. Put together a procedural one-sheet about labeling files for your staff. This seems completely OCD, but seriously, do it from the get-go. If you don't, you'll end up with some file folders that have client names, some that don't, some with codes, some without. It's a giant hassle you want to avoid. You can't believe how many ways there are to label something until you ask different people to do it without guidelines.

4. Make a note in your calendar for November 1st, and tag it "repeat yearly"—Make new folders for the next year.

Let the sorting begin. All receipts (yours and your staff's) and vendor invoices—this includes online orders, cash receipts, credit card receipts, check stubs, everything—will be collected, labeled by job code, and given to the bookkeeper for data entry and filing.

Hire a Bookkeeper

"Bookkeeper?" you ask in dismay. "You mean I have to spend money to hire an additional employee?" Yes, no matter how small the company, hiring a bookkeeper to come in at least part-time is a must. Why is this so important? Because even if they only come in once a week for a few hours, they will keep you on track. This person (if they are doing their job) will force you to actually turn in your receipts every week—your *coded* receipts. This person will make sure the staff's time is coded properly and turned in on time. Plus, I can't imagine that bookkeeping is exactly your strong suit. I haven't met many entrepreneurs who are jumping up and down dying to process payroll.

You, the big boss, need to be free to "see the forest." You should not be spending three hours a week entering data—it is not worth your time. As the boss, you need those three hours a week *to review* the data. The bookkeeper will take care of the "trees" by processing receipts and vendor invoices, entering them into the computer, balancing the company checkbook, sorting the timesheets and expenses by job code, and generating P&Ls (with back-up documentation, if necessary) for you to review.

One place where you can slide, though—the bookkeeper doesn't necessarily need to be an employee, an independent contractor is probably fine. Talk to your tax professional about that one. Whether you find someone on Craigslist or through a temp service, your bookkeeper is the person who will force you to make sure you're collecting the data, and get it into the system in a *timely* manner. We can all get it into the system at some point, it's the timeliness part I want you to work on.

Procedures for Timesheets, Receipts, Invoices and P&Ls

Here's a brief overview on how all this new data flows through the office.

Timesheets

1. Employee timesheets are turned in every day to the boss's inbox. You check them to see how your staff is spending its time. You check them *daily*—too many mistakes get made if you don't. Time passes and people don't remember things. After a week they can't recall if they were working on Terri's design project or Mary's invoices. By the way, make sure timesheets are signed and dated by both the employee (or contractor) and the boss.

2. Timesheets are routed from the boss to the bookkeeper, who enters the data in the computer by job code.

Receipts

1. Similarly, employees' receipts (job codes printed at the top) are turned in once a week to the boss's inbox for approval. (At The Party Goddess!, receipts are due on Mondays.) Once approved, the receipts are put in the bookkeeper's inbox.

2. When it comes to invoices, I'm thinking of them just like receipts. You might get a receipt from the office supply store but an invoice when you order something online. Same thing as far as I'm concerned. By whatever means you get the receipt or invoice, print it out, label it with the proper job code and give it to the bookkeeper.

3. The bookkeeper enters the receipts and invoices into Quickbooks (a dedicated accounting program), or whatever system you're using, stamps them "posted," then copies them. Originals are filed in vendor folders and copies are put in the appropriate client folders.

4. Special note: if a receipt is lost by an employee, there is no, I repeat, *no* reimbursement for that expense. If you want to be nicer than I am about this, knock yourself out. I recommend a very limited tolerance for this, or you're just asking for problems.

P&Ls

Have your bookkeeper, whether part-time or full-time, generate these job P&Ls for you on the following schedules (once you get the hang of things, you can adjust the frequency but don't get too slack—you'll regret it.) :

1. P&Ls for every project just closed (weekly)

2. P&Ls for open projects (weekly)

3. P&L for the previous month, along with the bank reconciliation (on or shortly after the 10th of the month. There is *no reason* this should be done later. No excuses—take my guidelines here to heart)

4. P&L for the year-to-date. If it's the middle of April, you would have the P&L for March on your desk. You'd also have a P&L for January through March (assuming you create your financial statements based on a calendar year, which I recommend). This will help you determine how you're tracking for the year. Are you meeting your sales goals? Profit margins? How's labor coming in overall?

OK, let's move forward. You understand expense coding, you've set up a new filing system, you've hired your bookkeeper. Now it's time to get your team on board with the plan.

Chapter 11
POW-WOW WITH YOUR PEEPS

Confrontation, rather, *communicating* with your employees is not always a ton of fun. However, you are about to change their world in a big way and you want this to go as smoothly as humanly possible. You've got to sit down and explain the nitty-gritty of how their work world is going to function from now on. It is important to let them know *why* you're implementing all of the changes associated with expense coding. It's not about them. It's about you, or you and your bottom line, which need to be firmly in synch, once and for all, from this day forward. And your bottom line ultimately becomes about them.

When you sit down with your staff, whether that staff is full-time, part-time or volunteer, pretend you're the kindergarten teacher and this is the first day of school. If you come across as a sloppy, wet noodle, they will walk all over you. Be strong, rehearse your lines and hold firm. You're only going to get one shot at a first impression, and this first impression is crucial.

GATHER THE TROOPS

OK, so *you're* finally getting it, but you, after all, are the boss. How exactly are you going to get *everyone else* on board with this new concept of job costing? Call a meeting, virtual or otherwise, yesterday. Ask your team if they've noticed that you just haven't been yourself lately—you're stressed out, fried, agitated and short-tempered. (They will all nod. In fact, they'll probably be brats and act like you've never been anything *but* stressed out, fried, agitated and short-tempered.) Ask them if they would like that to change? Would it be easier and more enjoyable for them to come to work if you were in a better mood, feeling more confident and actually able to pay them without totally stressing out? (The violent nodding will continue.) Perfect, you say, here's how we're going to do it. As a team, we are going to start—drum roll, please—revenue and expense coding. For the health of our company and your livelihood (remember, you always want to tie it back to *them* and what's beneficial to them—they aren't so concerned about what's beneficial to you), each of you will need to make some adjustments in the way you do things.

A Necessary Agenda

You will then outline the new job coding plan, explaining:

- The concept of Code Your Way to Cash and the rationale behind it. Briefly touch upon A, B, C and D costs.

- Job codes—how to create them. Whatever system you've set up— your clear-cut, transparent, easy to communicate, and simple to replicate system—whatever you've decided upon, here's where the rubber meets the road: you have to explain it to a group of people and make certain they can all do it. Without you watching.

- B Costs—everyone on the team is going to be responsible for completing a timesheet, complete with job codes, every single day. (Your peeps will gasp, stare and gape. This is a completely normal and expected reaction.) Hand out a blank timesheet to everyone, as well as a sample timesheet filled out by a make-believe employee of the company. Everyone will start tracking their time in fifteen-minute increments, assigning a job code and an activity to each chunk of time.

- A and C Costs—everyone will start tagging receipts and vendor invoices with job codes. (Introduce this concept, but it's easiest if the goal of this first meeting is to jumpstart the employee timetracking. Once that is running smoothing, hold another meeting to delve into how you will code receipts.)

- Physical changes to the office, such as the new filing system and inboxes/outboxes.

- How (and who) the new vendor and client folders will be created.

- What the labels will look like (present your nifty one-sheet on how to create the labels and in what format).

- How you will handle past projects, those in progress and the brand new ones coming in from this day forward. (For example, are you going create folders for jobs that are currently in progress, or solely for new jobs that arise from this day forward?)

- The role the (possibly new) bookkeeper plays in tracking and recording receipts.

- Policies and procedures for payroll and reimbursements.

DEFUSING THE BOMB

Walking into a lion's den when the lion might be sleeping is one thing. Walking into a pride of lions when you know they are awake, alert, hungry, caffeinated and with their friends is really unfortunate. I don't know about you, but that's how I feel talking to my employees sometimes (I'm including independent contractors and other regular team members in this group). Change is not always fun but in order to run a profitable business, you've got to course correct, constantly. And course correction involves sitting down with your staff and discussing what's working and what's not. As the leader, it's up to you to lay down the law, get buy-in from your team and hope they have enough trust in you to do it as cheerfully as possible. Hopefully, you've made enough deposits in those emotional bank accounts, as Stephen Covey likes to say.

Making the shift from total anarchy, rather, your old way of doing things, to running a tight ship with timetracking and coding, is a significant change. If you recognize this and try to see it from your staff's perspective, the shift will be a lot more comfortable for all involved. A good friend and colleague once told me that he always prefaces the mailing (or e-mailing) of a "negative" letter to a client with a phone call. He says this makes a world of difference in defusing the bomb. No one likes to open an envelope or an e-mail and have it explode in their lap. My colleague asserts that with a phone call, you're softening the blow and the recipient can hear your voice, ask questions, read your true, intended tone because you're actually talking to them. Bottom line? Anticipate that your new plan is going to take some getting used to, make sure you're fully fed before you sit down with everyone, and whatever you do, *turn your cell phone off.* Seriously, let your team know that their normally frazzled boss is committed to making positive changes. You want their total attention, so you must give them yours.

So here's what you might be in for. Employee reactions often include:

- What's wrong with the way we were doing things?

- Do you think we don't work hard enough?

- If we work faster, can we just do things the old way?

- Don't you trust us?

- This is going to take so much time!

Have your own plan to answer each of these questions *before* the meeting starts. You might even want to brainstorm a list of other objections that they might have. In effect, you're selling your team on your new approach, so *be prepared.* And at the end of the day, keep in mind, you are the boss. Your name is the one on the door, it is your responsibility to get the taxes paid and their paychecks to clear. I'm not saying to be completely unsympathetic to their objections, I'm just reminding you not to get bullied to back down. If you're going to be the boss, you're going to have to pull on your wading boots once in awhile.

- *Objection #1: What's wrong with the way we were doing things?*
  Nothing is really wrong with the way they were doing things. In fact, they were just following your direction (or lack thereof). But what's wrong now is that the company is not as profitable as it

should be and there are problems that need to be solved. Before they can be solved, the root of the problems needs to be identified. Through this new way of doing things, together you can isolate the source of the problems and then correct them.

- *Objection #2: Do you think we don't work hard enough?* I know how hard you all work and that's precisely why we are going to implement these new procedures. It's important that we are actually *benefiting* from all of the time you put in. I want to make the best, most efficient use of your time as possible. Once a task is completed, you can move on to something else that will improve our bottom line. By tracking our time and expenses this way, we can spend our time doing what's best for the bottom line of the company.

- *Objection #3: If we work faster, can we just do things the old way?* It's not about working faster, it's about working smarter. As a company, we are moving toward the same goal, and everyone needs to be rowing in the same direction. Expense coding is going to shed light on where we're *not* all rowing in the same direction, so that we can increase productivity. We want to minimize the angst and effort being put toward tasks or projects that don't make sense for the company.

- *Objection #4: Don't you trust us?* If I didn't trust you, you wouldn't be here. In fact, I trust you so much that I know you are all going to be amazing at this. In the end, you will feel a lot better about how you're spending your time. Together, we're going to cut costs and get more efficient, so we can focus on delivering the best service/product to our customers. The better, stronger and faster we're able to do that, the healthier the company is, the more job security you have, and the more rewarded we all will be. We might hit a few snags along the way, but we can handle those as they arise.

- *Objection #5: This is going to take so much time!* Initially, yes, this is going to take some time to implement, get used to and tweak.

But before you paint your house, you've got to strip it down and prime it. You have to take the time to do the prep work or you won't get that beautifully restored house. Maybe when we strip off the old paint, we'll find some termites and some damaged parts of the foundation. That's all right. We have to fix the core problems that were previously masked, address them, and then move on.

At the end of the day, put yourself in your staff's shoes. What do we all really want? To be heard, appreciated, respected and part of something that's great—whether it's a family, a business, a non-profit or a church. No one wants to be on a losing team that the other schools make fun of. Anticipate the objections, prepare your answers, sit with an open mind, listen, and course correct as you go. Hang in there, you're going to be fine.

B COSTS—THE PEEPS BEGIN TIMETRACKING

The day after you drop the Code Your Way to Cash bomb, follow up to make sure everyone is actually completing their timesheets. Play cheerleader throughout the day. Start by checking in mid-morning to ask how it's going and answer any questions that have bubbled up.

Do the same thing around lunchtime. Your peeps will say they haven't had time to fill out the timesheets. At this point, you sit down with them and make time. Pull out your stopwatch and demonstrate exactly how long it takes to complete a timesheet (about two minutes if you're really slow).

Rinse and repeat about thirty minutes before people start to leave at the end of the day. They will still be groaning. That's OK. Yes, you need to be babysitting them for the next couple of days. Not four times a day, but at least once. Hover! Be a helicopter parent! Let your peeps know you're watching. It's going to take them a little time to get used to diligent timetracking, but they will get it. Don't worry—no matter how much they complain, they won't die. As far as I know, nobody jumped on the Expense Coding Bus and keeled.

And you, the big boss, need to monitor the timesheets *every* day. By managing employee time on a daily basis, you can quickly course correct when problems arise. Note that timesheets must be signed by both the employee and boss, as it really is an agreement between the two of you that the employee has worked the hours he/she claims, and that you agree. While at first this may seem overwhelming, you will pick up speed and be able to hone in on the problem spots quickly. For The Party Goddess!, my company of five full-time employees, I spend about ten minutes per day monitoring timesheets and the job codes. Totally worth it, because how else would I have discovered that my staff had spent three hours of unbilled time researching a venue for a *potential* event? The client hadn't made the booking, but I had asked my staff to do the legwork, assigned the project a job code, which came through on their timesheets. I'll say it again—this was for an event we hadn't even booked. The light bulb went on.

Stuffing the Drawer No Longer

Now that you've got your staff on board and tracking their time, it's time for you set a plan for pinning down the rest of the details and costs associated with working on a particular project.

The first step: collecting receipts and vendor invoices. Since the goal is to track *all* the expenses related to a job, you must collect *all* receipts. Accuracy is crucial both for tax purposes and your pricing, which is based partially on your costs.

If you are audited by the IRS and don't have a back-up receipt or invoice, you might as well not even bother claiming it as an expense. The government doesn't consider an undocumented expense legitimate, and therefore neither should you.

If expenses are forgotten or improperly coded, not only will a specific job be underpriced, but subsequent jobs will be underpriced too. The health of your company depends on accuracy in collecting receipts. Plus, it's important that you send a message to your staff and vendors that you are reviewing your numbers and paying attention, not just signing checks and being lazy.

You and your staff have to become hyper-vigilant about collecting receipts for *everything* associated with the business. This means that, although it seems ridiculous, get that $0.50 receipt for parking. Every penny counts—at least at this point.

When anyone forgets to get a receipt, they need to go back to the vendor and get one—even if it's a hand-scribbled note on the back of the vendor's business card. You as the boss have to get tough about missing receipts: my policy, which I explain very clearly to my employees, is that if they forget a receipt, they do not get reimbursed for the expense. Believe me, if this happens once, it never happens again because they know how seriously I insist on having their receipts.

As soon as a receipt is handed over—to you or to any of your employees—it must be coded with five pieces of information: the name of the employee who made the purchase (initials are fine with me if they are OK with you), the job code, the client or project name, the purpose of the expense, and the expense category for the P&L (for The Party Goddess! expense categories might by "Décor" or "Crew Meals"). These should be written on the original receipt. My rule is that I don't leave the counter without doing this coding—it's easiest to do it immediately, when the transaction is fresh in my mind.

Sometimes the receipt or invoice is for a general expense, such as marketing. Even though it is not connected to a specific job, it should still be coded with the words "no code." Having no code is *not* an excuse for having no receipt. There is not an excuse for not writing a code or not writing "no code." Some acknowledgement is needed. A blank space where the code or "no code" notation should be signals the bookkeeper to investigate the expense. Did someone forget the code, or is there really "no code"? Leave no doubt!

Gone are the days of stuffing receipts into your drawer, purse, laptop case, and glove compartment. Collect them in one place, whether it's your wallet, a pocket in your purse, an envelope or a Ziploc bag. Find a system that works for you—one place to put your receipts—so that you can finish processing them.

For the employees, processing means turning in coded receipts and invoices to the boss for approval. This is a fluid process that goes on throughout the day. Hard copies are put into the boss's inbox. Online purchases can be handled as they occur. For example, an employee is tasked with ordering a client gift online. She scouts out the possibilities, finds the option, shoots an e-mail to the boss requesting approval (if needed), then purchases the gift. The online confirmation is forwarded to the bookkeeper, with the five pieces of information coded at the top of the e-mail. (Note that you may want to implement the use of an expense report for activities such as travel, in which there will be lots of receipts for a single project or activity. You don't have to, but it is something to consider—many larger companies usually do this.)

When you first start to Code Your Way to Cash, you will want to approve every receipt, until you are certain that your employees understand the new system. Yes, sorry, you are not only approving timesheets every day, here's something else you need to approve. My employees request approval by putting their receipts in my inbox or by sending me an e-mail or fax (I know it's a little antiquated and my husband thinks this is one of the dumbest habits I have, but I still like some things faxed because I want to touch and write on the paper. Electronic copies don't always do it for me. But that kind of minutiae is up to you.) I signal approval by initialing a hard copy or fax, or by e-mail for requests made online. If an employee turns in an expense report, the boss is effectively approving all of the receipts at the same time. Approved receipts are then routed to the bookkeeper, via the bookkeeper's inbox or e-mail.

To summarize, receipts come in from five sources:

- They are collected by the boss and employees at point of sale.

- They come in as electronic confirmation for online ordering.

- They come by fax.

- They come by snail mail.

- They come via courier or delivery person who makes you sign for the package delivered to your door.

The boss approves every receipt or vendor invoice before its next stop: the bookkeeper's inbox, where it's processed for payment.

The Bookkeeper Tidies Up

We are now ready to talk about the bookkeeper's role in processing receipts. All receipts and invoices have been coded, approved, and funneled in her direction. Every time the bookkeeper comes in to the office, even if that's only once a week, she processes them.

The bookkeeper sorts receipts and invoices by type of payment: cash, debit and credit cards, PayPal and checks, and any other way you can pay for something. After confirming that every receipt is properly coded (and if a receipt isn't properly coded, she goes back to the person who processed it for payment), she enters the data into the computer system. She may use software like QuickBooks or simply an Excel spreadsheet. The expenses will be organized by job and then by expense category within job.

Once entered in the system, a receipt is stamped "posted." The bookkeeper photocopies the receipts: she files originals by specific vendor name (or "Miscellaneous A" if the vendor is not frequent enough to warrant their own file), and files copies in the job folder for that job. Receipts that are coded "no code" are also placed in the vendor file (these don't need to be copied, copies are only for job files).

For reimbursable expenses that employees have incurred, you need to have a system for payment. In my company, reimbursements are generally paid twice a month with payroll. However, if an employee has forked over her own money for a significant expense ("significant" by the employee's definition of the word), early payment can be requested, which will be made the next time the bookkeeper is in the office. (If you aren't sensitive to this, the next time you're in a pinch and ask her to run out and buy stamps, she will protest because she knows it will take too long to process the reimbursement and she can't tie up her cash like that.) Once the reimbursement check is cut, the receipt is then attached to the employee's check stub, and filed in the employee's vendor file (yes, each member of your staff will have a vendor file).

Receipt by receipt and invoice by invoice, the bookkeeper processes everything turned in that week, and especially everything associated with current jobs. When the bookkeeper prints a P&L for current jobs or those that were closed out the previous week, the boss can analyze what went right and what went wrong, and adjust accordingly.

Isn't It Fun Being In Charge?

So now what? You've got to keep everyone on a really short leash at first. They will continue to thrash and moan and complain a blue streak. You will be convinced that employee morale is going to tank. Maybe they will quit. That's OK if they do. There is a new sheriff in town and it's high noon.

Chapter 12

EVALUATE THE DATA IN LIGHT OF THE THREE BIG QUESTIONS

The dust is settling and the picture isn't pretty. Your bottom line is probably a little less sweet than you thought. Let's face it—this is going to sting a bit. But you have to go through that stinging pain to get beyond it to the other side. Might as well rip the Band-Aid off now; you'll have to do it sooner or later anyway.

ALL SYSTEMS GO

Life in the office is different now. New systems are in place. The staff is reluctantly tracking time on the dreaded timesheets. They are also grumpily coding receipts and funneling them through you for approval and on to the bookkeeper. The bookkeeper is recording all the numbers, filing receipts in the appropriate folders or binders—collecting all the information you need to Code Your Way to Cash.

Let the machine run for a few weeks. Allow time for some data to come in. You'll be checking timesheets nightly during this period (and making any necessary adjustments based on what you see), but you can't really do a job cost analysis until you've completed some projects, or are at least well into them.

GRADUATING FROM EXPENSE CODING 101

Time to get real. Yes, my friend, it's time to use your P&Ls and actually Code Your Way to Cash. Take three projects, preferably significant ones, and ask your bookkeeper to give you the P&L *for each project*. The projects don't have to be finished, but they must be well in progress. Take the P&Ls, and find yourself a quiet space in which you will not be interrupted for two hours. Make it clear to your staff that you are unavailable—"It will just take a minute" always takes at least five, or twenty-five if you're me. I recommend you do not allow yourself near your computer or phone, because when your brain gets stuck, it's too easy to distract yourself by answering e-mails and calls or posting that tempting Tweet, instead of forging ahead with the task at hand.

Get out your paper and pencil and get ready to make notes. Sit down, put up your feet, and examine these P&Ls.

ANALYZE THIS

Sample *Job* Profit and Loss Statement (P&L):

Client/Project:	Job Code:
Wince's Birthday	12D11A

Revenue: $ 5,000.00

Expenses:

Food	1,500.00
Beverages	400.00
Staff Labor	1,000.00
Rentals	400.00
Signage/Printing	320.00
Shipping	80.00
Travel/Mileage	100.00
Total Expenses	(3,800.00)

Net Profit/Loss: $ 1,200.00

The difference between total income and total expenses:
$5,000 - $3,800 = $1,200

What do you notice? You will see your A Costs, B Costs, and C Costs for each job. The first thing to do is make sure every number on those P&Ls is accurate. Do you have any questions? Does a particular figure look out of place—way too high, or way too low? For example, if printing costs are twice what you'd expect them to be, go back and double check the supporting documents make sure they actually are correct. Perhaps an invoice was coded incorrectly and you are indeed seeing costs for another job on this P&L. Make sure every number is accurate before you move on. When I say every number, I don't mean every single cent. If it's pretty close, move on. It's more important that you practice and get the hang of it than for you to balance every single penny.

Now, quick and dirty, what do you see? What jumps out at you? Are you shocked by how much time it took to research that product? Are you surprised by how much you spent on shipping? Didn't you realize there were set-up charges? Order minimums that needed to be met? A contractor that charged for drive time? Somebody's billing you for mileage at twice the rate you normally pay?

Look closely at all three P&Ls, making notes of what you see. This is where enlightenment happens and things get really interesting. "Aha!" you say. "I can't believe that we spent four (insert bold expletive) hours picking up those samples! Where were we going, Acapulco?" Or, "Since when does Terri charge us to *drive* to the office to spend the day with us on a project? Has she always done that? Have I always paid for that? Does *everyone* charge me to drive?" Which leads to the sickening thought: "Oh no, what if the others find out I've been paying Terri to drive in. They'll want to be paid as well, and maybe for driving in the past. In fact, I'll go broke paying retroactive mileage accruals!" Maybe you aren't as dramatic as I am, but that's how the conversations typically go in my head. One Aha! leads to another. These are the leaks through which the money is pouring out of the dam of your business. Pouring, gushing, trickling, it's heading in the wrong direction. You've got to plug the dike, pronto.

How? Start asking yourself: What repeats? Where are there similarities? You can be sure that certain patterns are going to emerge again and again. Why? Well, because when you have a particular type of business, you'll see the same thing happening over and over. It won't necessarily be the same thing that happens to someone else in another type of business—you need to find your unique set of problem spots. Dig in—once you see those problems, you can start to do something about them. Write them down, and get ready to consider them in light of the Big Three Questions.

THE BIG THREE QUESTIONS

When you're in Africa on a safari, it's all about the "Big Five." If you return from your über-fab vacation having spotted the Big Five (lion, elephant, Cape buffalo, leopard, and rhino, in case you're interested), you've got your hunting trophy. In expense coding, it's the Big Three. Basic though they are, the Big Three Questions will lead you to the pot of gold. Throughout your business life, you will visit them again and again. These questions are about finding the money between the wallpaper and the wall, and expanding that gap by asking:

- Can I raise my prices?

- Can I cut expenses?

- How can I be more efficient?

Yes, you have another mantra: Can I raise my prices? Can I cut my expenses? How can I be more efficient? (If you really want to be one of my warriors, you can later change the first question to: "*How* can I raise my prices?" This question is the most controversial and perhaps difficult to swallow.)

QUESTION ONE—CAN I RAISE MY PRICES?

First, does your company offer something that no one else does? If yes, you can probably charge more. If no, could you make it *seem* like your product or service is drastically different from the competition's in order to charge more? Are you sure that you're exploiting all of your brand's amazing virtues? All of your own differential advantages? Come on, start making a list. We've all got something we could pimp out a little more. Can you make your client *want* your product or service rather than just *need* it, so that your client is driven by emotion, not price? Or could you make it so they could want or need it a little more often? Re-examine your marketing and see if you can *create a more emotional buy.*

Do a little market research. What is the competition charging? This is important to look at regularly—I recommend you do it at least twice a year. Put "check out the competition" into your calendar so that you keep up with the current market conditions in your industry. Type in "repeat every six months." Do this homework regularly, and the operative word here is *do*. Not think about, try to get to, promise to consider, but *do*.

There are all sorts of ways to raise your prices without making them seem higher to your clients. For example, can you add a service charge to what you do? A delivery fee? Change fees? Additional labor line items? Installation and strike charges? Overtime clauses? Get creative!

Remember what we learned from our friend Anna the stylist? If you can't raise your prices across the board and you're convinced that your additional line items are intact, could you add parameters to some of them? For example, could you charge $100 for delivery (or installation and strike—whatever your industry term is for delivery) within a ten-mile radius and $150 if the location is more than ten miles away? Could you charge extra for delivery on a weekend or during rush hour? Customers are often willing to pay extra to have something delivered at a set time instead of waiting around all day (like we all do when it comes to the never-on-time cable guy). If you clearly offer options to your customers as additional services you provide, you're effectively raising your prices without actually saying, "Guess what? I'm now doubling the old rate.

There's also the concern about upsetting existing clients with a rate hike. Perhaps you can you raise your prices for new clients, but keep your existing clients at the old structure for several months until you can get the word out that rates are going up. If you make the determination that you have been undercharging for far too long and need to make a change, then lay out a plan for explaining the new pricing to your customers. Personalize it with a follow-up phone call if you can, at least to your most valued customers. Explain *why* your prices are going up: "You have probably seen the newspaper headlines of the steadily rising gas prices . . . " or "With our workers' compensation premiums doubling since we first went into business . . . " Then explain the benefit to the customer for continuing to work with you: "Because we want to continue to ensure timely deliveries . . . " or " . . . it's crucial that we maintain adequate insurance coverage for the safety and peace of mind of you, our customers."

Business changes, costs change and markets fluctuate. If you've been providing excellent service or products up to this point, your customers will understand and want to stay with you. If, however, you've been slacking off for a while, and send a letter saying that the cost of doing business with you just increased by 40%, you'll need another book of advice to bail you out of that one.

Question Two—Can I Cut Expenses?

Examine your biggest expense category or categories and start thinking about what you can do. What is *your* biggest expense category? It's different for every business.

Some service businesses like accounting firms or law offices operate with high labor expenses or time—the Bs. Other businesses like Julia and her design company have a healthy combination of both. She's got lots of A Costs in terms of her Cost of Goods Sold, the costs of the physical product she sells. In addition, she's got a support team that has to get that product to market, her Bs. And she has all those hidden costs, her Cs.

After running through a few sample projects to practice your expense coding skills, you'll start to see the patterns (there's that word again, *pattern*) emerging in your own set of circumstances. And once you've mastered the art of finding the patterns, you're on the road to success because you'll be able to spot areas that need improvement and course correct. It's that rapid course correction that really starts to save you money.

One of the ways you can save money is to start shopping for new vendors. Now I can already *hear* the objections: "But there's nobody else that can provide that quality of product!" Or, "I've worked with that vendor for years; he is struggling just like I am. I can't bail on him now!" Note that I said *start shopping* for new vendors. I did not say, "Now go and switch vendors." Knowledge is power. I want you to get educated. Start investigating and put down the tissues. You're going to be fine.

Begin by interviewing your existing vendors. Tell them that you are embarking on a major efficiency campaign. You're looking to cut your expenses, lean out and tighten up your whole operation, and are starting by interviewing your key, favorite, most valued vendors. Have a dialogue. Ask if they offer price breaks at a certain point that you're not taking advantage of. Could you avoid delivery charges altogether if you received orders on a certain day or at a certain time? Could you get lower prices by piggybacking on to other customers' orders? Ask open-ended questions so that they can be part of your solution. They can probably cook up some original ideas that you never would have thought of.

Next, investigate new vendors entirely. Again, not telling you to switch just yet. But learn about how they price. Are there specials you would be eligible for as a new customer? What would that company be willing to throw in to earn your business? See what kind of incentives they could offer you, or you could offer them. Maybe you could get preferred pricing if you referred them a certain amount of new business. Look for the win-win.

You get the drift. It's like corridor thinking. Picture yourself at one end of a long hall and you're trying to get to the doorway facing you at the end of the hall. That's your goal. As you head towards that door you notice a few other open doors. Maybe you peer into one or another of them. Guess what? On your way to your goal, you found something more appealing, more inspiring, cheaper, better—you get it. The point is that you wouldn't have encountered it had you not headed down that corridor toward your goal. By identifying what you're after or where you're going, you often find the answer on the way, albeit in a different form than what you'd originally imagined.

What I've learned is that whatever you measure starts improving. I wish I knew why. It seems that all you have to do is start tracking— whether it's labor, expenses or widgets— and you become more efficient.

Everything and everyone starts tightening up and then, my friend, you start finding that money between the wallpaper and the wall.

QUESTION THREE—HOW CAN I BE MORE EFFICIENT?

Examine every line item on your P&Ls (your job P&Ls and your monthly P&Ls) and ask where you can be more efficient. Oh, you're thinking, efficiency, that means time—the B Costs. Yes, it does mean the B Costs, but not *just* the B Costs. And don't you dare tell me that you can't be more efficient. Everyone, repeat, everyone can be more efficient somehow. Marathon runners beat their own personal best all the time. What's your personal best? I don't care what it is, just beat it.

Actually, a lot of your work to make your staff more efficient with their time has already been done because you've been inspecting the timesheets every night. You've been catching lapses in efficiency for weeks now. Now, as you look over the P&Ls, you can see the aggregate of your and your staff's time for the particular project you're examining (listed as "Staff Time," or "Outside Services" if you're using a virtual team member). If a time line item is way out of whack, go back to the timesheets for greater clarity.

And, of course, once you've seen where everyone's time is going, you can think about how to use their time more wisely. Perhaps you can actually charge more for time by creating parameters to account for that time—time for traveling, walk-throughs, in-person meetings—when you write your contracts. Or maybe you could have a lower person on the totem pole handle certain tasks. Get creative—the options are endless.

Some smart event planners I know charge a flat fee to coordinate events, but use parameters for their contracts so they don't end up earning ten cents an hour at the hands of a high maintenance client. These planners might charge $7,000 to coordinate an event, and then spell out exactly what that $7,000 includes—i.e., two in-person meetings no more than ninety minutes long, timeline creation, and so on. You get the picture. Parameters can also be used to state what the $7,000 would *not* include, or would be available for an additional fee—i.e., invitation design, 24/7 psychological counseling. (You think I'm joking.)

Where is your staff's time going? Maybe they are spending a lot of time answering questions that are asked over and over again (even things as simple as directions or where to park). Why not create an in-depth "Frequently Asked Questions" section on your website that you can refer clients to? You could even include a FAQs page in your proposals.

Make sure you have set up procedures for everything your business does on a regular basis. The guidelines for these procedures: they should be easy to understand, replicable and accessible. Then make sure that everyone in your company understands and agrees to those procedures. There should be a universal way to do everything from answering the phone to preparing proposals to closing the sale.

Other efficiency questions you should ask as you view the P&Ls are connected to the A and C Costs. Are you seeing lots of rush charges? How about repeated orders for the same item, when you could save money if you ordered in bulk? Are you spending money on overtime? You will start *planning* more carefully in order to avoid unnecessary expenses.

You've got to start improving efficiency somewhere, so start digging in and looking for those patterns. Everything you need is contained in the data you already have. You just have to use it!

Bonus Question Four—Can I Sell More?

This is a tempting but dangerous option at this point in the game. For now, we are talking about improving your bottom line through job costing, not through expansion of your business. Remember how busy you already are? Expanding the business will just make you more stressed and busier, but you will still be losing money if you are not tracking your expenses per project and running your business by those scorecards.

Right now we are tightening your belt. Put all of your focus on determining where you are, and how much you are currently making doing things the way you've always done them. You're in the process of implementing huge changes. Keep your focus on your new process, running the new systems, and taking the time to Code Your Way to Cash.

If you were also to try to focus on selling more, you would start spinning your wheels like crazy, and ultimately those wheels would come off the bus. Plus there's the added danger: increased sales can mask problems. Some of the biggest problems in my company occurred when I had the greatest sales. Why? Because when money is flowing in fast and furiously and you're making payroll with no stress, you get lazy. You slack off on those little things you used to do to monitor your expenses and save time and money. Unfortunately, the fat and happy times can be the beginning of the end if you don't keep some of that hubris in check. That's why I don't want you going after more sales. Lean out before you bulk up, or as a good friend of mine says, "Slow down so you can speed up."

"Souping" Up the P&L

Back to your three sample P&Ls. If you could repeat those projects, what would you do differently? Review your list of Aha! moments, your red flags, the problems specific to you and your business. Think about the Big Three Questions, and for every red flag, brainstorm an idea for change and write it down. There are all sorts of ideas to explore. Solutions may not only be about saving money, but also about negotiating terms, choosing a new vendor, or possibly outsourcing certain aspects of the business. This list of ideas is your prescription for improving the bottom line, your pathway to making more money.

Don't Get Mad, Get Impartial

Sometimes it can be very upsetting to realize that you've made the same mistake again and again (it can also be upsetting to realize you've made a mistake just once and it cost you thousands of dollars!). For example, you might notice that you personally are keeping FedEx in business because you're always overnighting things to clients. With a little more planning, those charges wouldn't be necessary, or could certainly be reduced. So, get mad for a minute, then shake it off and ask what you can do better. Grab on to your objectivity. The more impartial you are with your evaluation, the more effective you can be in moving forward.

All this "bad news" has been out there since you've been running your business. The only difference now is that you *know* it. It's feedback, after all, and it's neither positive nor negative. It's simply information. Looking at what happened with a healthy degree of detachment allows you to make better decisions.

There is so much to learn about creating a profitable company. You have to dissect your business objectively and honestly to figure out what it is that you've got to learn. Expense coding enables you put on your lab coat and goggles and do the dissection. You can then authentically—scientifically, even—evaluate what is working for you and what isn't. The healthy parts of your business will be exposed, as well as the money sinkholes. Then you can take action, stop what's not working, and concentrate on growing the profitable segments of your business.

Chapter 13

WE'VE ALL BEEN THERE

Welcome to the wonderful world of job costing. I know, the terrain is unfamiliar and even kind of scary. But don't worry—others have blazed the trail before you and you can benefit from their experience. Let's take a look at some common issues. It's always helpful to know that you are not alone.

PERMISSION GRANTED—HOW TO CHARGE FOR THE EXTRAS

Many small business owners don't have the confidence to charge what they're worth. They underbid and undersell themselves 24/7, and the end result is not so good. When you finally discover all of those hidden costs, you have facts upon which you can make price adjustments—actual knowledge instead of just a gut feeling. When you really start understanding just how high your expenses are, it's a no-brainer to adjust your fees to cover them.

There is an uncomfortable period in which you have to tell old clients that your fees have increased. However, you now have the facts to back up that change. My experience is that when an increase is explained beforehand, backed up with facts that the clients can understand (i.e., higher delivery fees caused by increased gas prices), the client usually accepts it without any issues. The trouble arises when your best customer is midway through a project with you and (oops!) you forgot to mention that you now charge extra for all of the things they are used to getting for free.

There is a delicate balance in how you present the fees to the client, however. While the job's P&L contains all the back-up information and is totally specific, the client's invoice is not. If every single teeny tiny cost were put on the invoice, the client would feel nickeled and dimed and get very peeved very fast. How to avoid this? *You present the charges on an invoice by bundling them together.*

My rule of thumb for invoicing? Provide enough information so that it makes sense, but not so much that the client gets overwhelmed. There is a happy medium and it's definitely worth your time to find it. Now, this is true for both C Costs (hidden expenses) and B Costs (time). If a client questions a charge, you can confidently answer the query because you'll be so comfortable with your numbers. You won't stand there stammering, you'll really know *why* you're charging what you're charging and why you can't charge any less. If you're in doubt, you can always reference your P&Ls to see if you've got any room to negotiate on a particular line item. There's no harm in taking a second look, but don't react and immediately lower a price just because you get a little pushback. One thing helps me: when a customer asks me for a quote on the spot or to lower a particular line item, I ask if I can get back to them. There's something about taking a little time to think and not react in the moment that helps me make better decisions. The customer has every right to question how you charge them, you don't need to get defensive, you do need to get educated. However you choose to bundle the costs, including them is *crucial*, both to getting paid and to maintaining a strong repeat client base.

Some examples of how to bundle the costs together on the invoice? Meet Paul the photographer who is skillfully expense coding and pricing his jobs appropriately. He needs to be equally skillful when putting together his invoices. Let's say Paul needs a special camera lens for a particular job. He has to rent the lens and send his assistant to and from the camera shop twice, first to get the lens and then to return it. The cost of the lens really includes the rental fee, and the assistant's time and mileage. However, the invoice to the client reads simply: "Camera Lens Rental."

Similarly with Coco the event planner. Aware of all the hidden expenses, Coco knows that invitations cost a lot more than just printing and postage. They also include the calligrapher's fee, the employee's time to drop off and pick up the invitations from the calligrapher's house, and the assembly fee. (Yes, even if you take the invitations home and stuff them while watching TV, assembly takes time, and therefore, is not free! Just ask yourself: If my mother/sister/I were not stuffing and stamping these invitations and I had to hire someone to do it, what would a realistic cost be? Hourly or per piece doesn't matter, you need the going rate.) However, the client doesn't need to see each of these charges as a single line item. Coco bundles all the charges together and the invoice reads: "Invitations (Printing, Postage and Assembly)." The only situation in which a minor charge might be detailed on the invoice is if is to be discounted (section on discounts coming up!). For example, Coco decides to comp the assembly fee. Then, she definitely notes it as a line item and indicates that that expense was comped.

When you start charging fair fees because you understand the hidden costs of a job, you reap the benefits in two ways. Of course your profit margin will increase. In addition, your clients will respect you more when they see that you place a fair monetary value on your own services.

DISCOUNTS ARE GIFTS

On to discounts—a common pitfall. We've all been there. We've all gone out of our way to accommodate a client—we've discounted our rates, comped charges, and silently eaten the costs. After all we've given, the client makes an off-hand remark and we realize that they have no clue about how much we've done for them for free *already*! They've come to expect that our "fabulous rate" is not a gift, but simply our low price. We end up feeling a little bit abused and a lot angry.

In reality, we shouldn't be upset with the client because the fault lies within ourselves. We haven't educated the client about how much we've done for them. Therefore, our discounts and comps go unnoticed.

However uncomfortable you may be pointing it out, you can't let your actions go without thanks from the client. When you decide to give a discount or a comp, you will absorb a financial hit to your profit margin. To counterbalance that hit, you need to be sure that you get the benefit of the client's appreciation. If the client is grateful, they will come back for more business.

How do we make sure the client understands what we've done for them? *We point it out by showing it in writing. Every discount extended to a client should be noted as "comped" on the invoice.* This is the only way that the client will understand that you've actually given them a gift. By giving the gift, then pointing it out, you demonstrate attentive customer service and breed client loyalty. It also reduces the possibility of the client asking for more discounts, because you can point to the discounts you've already given them and justify why you can't take any more money off their invoice. If you don't note the comps on the invoice, but only inform the client about them when they ask for more discounts, you will appear to be disingenuous.

Underbidding Will Destroy You in the End

Have you ever noticed that when somebody new gets into your area of business, they often start getting a slew of clients by underbidding all of their competitors (you included)? You, the guy who's been around forever, get very hot under the collar. What is this new kid trying to do, put us all out of business? Is he *stupid*? Doesn't he realize this lame plan is going to come back and bite us all in the tush? All of the competition that has been around for ages gets their knickers in a knot because they are feeling the pain in their pocketbook.

After the pain, the fear sets in. Let's make our new kid on the block—we'll call him Cullen—a designer of vinyl decals and wall stickers. Now that Cullen is offering rock bottom prices, we realize that we're all going to have to lower our prices just to compete. This is horrible! Not so fast. Take a breath, relax, calm down.

How can I remain calm, you ask, when my world is crumbling down now that this newfound loser has entered the mix? Just wait. Let Cullen go ahead and undercut everyone. What will happen? The same thing that always does. The marketplace isn't stupid. *People don't shop on price alone.*

Yes, in the beginning everyone will lose a little business. Clients who are just price shoppers might try out the new kid in town to see what he's all about and some of those early customers will even be pretty happy with him. Cullen, Mr. Star Businessman, will be flattered and thrilled on many levels:

1. He's managed to steal some business away from the old-timers.

2. He's flattered that he can just open his doors and everyone flocks to him.

3. The money is rolling in.

But just like the restaurant that opens up and is packed for the first few weeks while everyone tries it out, then goes bust, Cullen's vinyl business will ultimately collapse. Why? Because Cullen has fallen into a trap. He blew into town from another area, a good designer with a decent track record as a business owner. However, he didn't know the new market and decided to take the easy way out. Instead of doing lots of market research and figuring out what kind of pricing the market would bear, or—better yet—instead of considering what opportunities existed in the marketplace that no one else was addressing, he got lazy. He figured he'd just charge less and make a splash. At the end of the day, however, Cullen got too busy too fast. While the first round of customers that flocked to him got really good service, the second round weren't as happy.

Cullen got overwhelmed. What started out as a great idea turned into his biggest nightmare—working all the time for ever more demanding clients. Things started to slip. In the midst of all of his busy-ness, Cullen lost focus. One customer's images were printed on the wrong vinyl, but he didn't handle the complaint. That should have been a simple issue to resolve, but Cullen didn't have time because he was already off servicing a new customer. The first customer, none too pleased at needing his product in time for the trade show and unable to get a return phone call or e-mail, decided to stop payment on his check. Cullen was too distracted to notice. Things went from bad to worse. The customer badmouthed Cullen all over town. Word got out. Potential customers who had heard about the new guy offering a great product and a great service at an unbeatable price started to get a little nervous. Some of them decided that they just didn't want to take a chance on Cullen's spotty service no matter how good his prices.

Without a clear differential advantage beyond cheap prices, Cullen was viewed as the town flake and, worse, had a reputation to match. When those customers who had originally jumped ship decided that Cullen wasn't as fabulous as they had originally thought, the old standby competitors were ready and waiting to service them.

So what's the moral of this story? You got it—*you can't compete on price alone.* (Unless you're Target or Wal-Mart, who both have made competing in the lower price marketplace one of their unique selling propositions. Low prices *can* be your differential advantage if you back them up with a consistent and basic level of service. Is Target's service as wondrous as you would find at Neiman Marcus? Of course not, but you're not paying Neiman's prices either.)

DITCH THAT DUMMY

Now that you are job costing, you will see that some jobs just do not have high profit margins. Have the confidence to walk away from these kinds of jobs—they are not worth your time. Seriously. Right now. Make a commitment. *Walk away.* In fact, hand-feed them to your competitors. If you can't make money on certain projects because your competition has underbid you, then guess what? Let them have it! Let them struggle and strain and answer the cockadoodle-doo client's calls at 7:00 p.m. and on Saturday mornings. Remember that high maintenance people who shop on price alone are not worth having as clients. They take away from the time you have for really good clients with healthy profit margins.

A few years ago, I decided to stop taking jobs for events under a certain dollar amount. Why? Because, as I once heard someone say, I wanted to look forward to the phone ringing again. My business had grown to where I was busy, busy, busy. So busy, all the time. Wasn't this just great? Everything I had ever dreamed about, right? I was the envy of all of the neighbors. My parents were proud. Their friends would say, "Oh, look at Marley, you must be so proud! She's everywhere, she's just so busy!" Um yeah. I was busy all right. Busy chasing my tail. One day I realized that if this "was all there was," I wasn't interested. I just didn't want to be that busy. I actually wanted to *make some money.* It's one thing to be so busy you forget your middle name when your bank account is overflowing. It's another thing to be working nonstop and trying to make sure your bank account isn't overdrawn in the morning. That's when it's not fun. In fact, it's stupid.

Enough was enough. I didn't want to work every Saturday night anymore, just so that I could say I was booked solid. Who wanted to be booked solid if I wasn't booking *profitable* business? I decided to raise my prices and implement a minimum. And I haven't looked back since.

We all get so caught up in the moment of wanting the sale, craving the deposit that we lose sight of the fact that getting business at all costs is not worth it. In fact, you're better off *not* taking business that's going to pull you down.

SOMETIMES IT'S OK TO HANG ON

On the other hand . . . sometimes there's a good reason to continue with aspects of your business that don't have high profit margins. For example, several years ago I deliberately decided to continue doing invitations for events although they are not a great source of profit (in fact, sometimes I lose money on invitations).

Through job costing, I realized that there are many reasons we don't make much money on invitations. They are incredibly labor-intensive. There is a lot of time spent going back and forth with the client on the wording, the design, and the proofing— it's actually quite tedious to get them right. I saw that we were taking in $200 on the invitation design, and my staff had spent five hours on the first round of proofs. I looked at those numbers and said, "No, no, no, no, and no." I realized I had a decision to make about my business. Although I loved the creative aspects of doing invitations, they didn't make money for the company. I had several options:

1. Stop doing invitations.

2. Find a more efficient way to do them.

3. See if there was anything else I needed to consider.

And so I considered. My gut told me that ditching the invitations wasn't as cut and dried as maybe the numbers portrayed. Why? Because we are a full-service catering and event planning company, and we pitch ourselves as a one-stop shop—it's integral to our marketing. Come to me with a date and a budget, and I will handle every single aspect of that event. I worried that if I didn't do the invitations, someone else would. Not only that, the client could go to another event planner who would say, "Hey, no problem. They don't want to do your invitations? I'll do your invitations, your cake, your décor, everything!"

I stared at everyone's timesheets, and asked myself if it would be worth losing a client over the invitations. The answer was no. Maybe I'd lose $100 here and there, but at least I'd be aware of it and I'd understand why I was making that choice. And it was a *choice,* instead of just going with blind faith, because I was armed with information. I knew what I was doing and *why* I was doing it.

I had a chat with my staff. I said, "We are not making money on invitations. We are doing them because we want to retain and satisfy our clients and you need to be as efficient as possible. Everybody got it?" They did.

I decided to amend my contract by saying to our clients, "Here is the price for these invitations. *It includes one round of changes. Each additional change will be billed at this hourly rate.*" By doing this, we built in a way to charge the customer for extra time that might be incurred when working on the invitations. We had protected ourselves if some high maintenance bride went rogue.

Consciously, *deliberately,* I would continue to create invitations for clients because being a one-stop shop would ultimately pay off. I also realized my marketing should focus on and promote the aspects of my business I enjoyed most and that were most profitable.

Trust Your Gut

After getting clear about who my ideal client was, I actually fired one. He started out like lots of them do, gung ho and *so* excited to work with me—excited to work with me as long as I would cut my prices. In retrospect, I don't think it was even about my fees, it was about the power struggle to "get me down." Here's the catch: his was a sizable job and worth my time, but the client was a lame-o and I had a gut feeling that if he was hammering me about price so early on in the game, it was not going to end well. So I fired him

I didn't say he was fired, of course! I said, "This is not a good fit." He was shocked. What? How could I, the service provider, announce that he, king of clients, was not a good fit? I needed the money, but it had started to feel too much like prostitution. It felt like I had to sell myself to pay the bills and I just couldn't stomach it. Not with this guy. He ranted and raved for about a week. But I didn't care. I was done.

And guess what? The week after I fired that client, I was hired for one of the biggest jobs in my career to date. *That* client and I are still friends today and that project was one of the most creative I've ever done. In fact, I still do interviews about that project and all of its creative elements.

And you know what? I would never have been able to accept this crazy fabulous client if I hadn't ditched lame-o. I had the foresight to know that in the long run, he wasn't right for me (just like dating!) and I certainly didn't want to build my business around someone like that. Call it energy, karma, juju, whatever you want—I didn't want vibes like that anywhere near me.

Donations

"Would you be willing to provide a donation for our Silent Auction? It's for a great cause!" How many times do we hear this request? Since The Party Goddess! is an event planning company, we are often asked to provide food for non-profit events: "Can you provide one hundred hors d'oeuvres for the museum's gala opening?" Now, the main reason you would ever respond "yes" is because you believe in and want to support the cause. Job costing will show you that the cost of doing so is higher than you think, and the incremental business that results may or may not ever offset those costs, as you will see below.

I would think to myself, "What's the cost of one hundred hors d'oeuvres, and are we going to get business out of this?" In the old days, I would inevitably agree to participate in the charitable event, thinking, "That donation of food will cost me a couple hundred bucks. Fine. It's a good cause." Later, I'd ask myself, "Now what was the business that I got because of the hors d'oeuvres I donated? I can't remember any of that business *actually coming in.*" Then I started expense coding.

The light dawned. The food for that charitable event cost $200, maybe. And I had to pay Angelica to go work the three-hour event. She had to set up, clean up, drive there, pack and unpack the truck, and go to a walk-through meeting ahead of time. Easily eight hours of her time. I tally up staff time, the e-mails, the meetings and everything else. There's another $80 because I created a flower arrangement so our table would look good. I also had to bring my guy in to wash the dishes and platters and finish all those random activities afterwards. Cha-Ching, Cha-Ching.

There was one charitable event in particular that we had done every single year because I believed in the cause—helping underprivileged children. I was already deceiving myself by thinking I got business out of it. When I did my expense coding after the event, our costs came to $2,100! Swear to you on my life, that was the cost—my *wholesale* cost, not what I would have charged *retail* if it were an actual, non-charitable event. Mind you, that didn't even take my time into consideration! How many cold calls could I have made to grow my business during the time I spent preparing for that event?

I almost had a heart attack. I kept adding it up thinking, "There's no way this is right." I double-checked and triple-checked the numbers. I completely freaked out. (Should I say that again? I was shocked and mortified.)

The next year the charity called, and I was reluctant to participate. I said to myself,

"You know what? I didn't particularly get business out of it, but it's not necessarily their fault. Sometimes that's just what happens with these things." I said, "Guess what? I ran my numbers last year. It cost me $2,100 to do your event." They of course said, "Oh, that's not possible." I told them, "Believe me, it's very possible because I ran the numbers ten times. But guess what? I love your organization. I will write you a check for $500." They were ecstatic! $500 free and clear, no strings attached? Worked for me too. I was still up $1,600. I made out like a bandit, and I got an ad in the program to boot.

Finding the Geese that Lay the Golden Eggs

While not directly connected to job costing and the scope of this book, you should be spending some time thinking about how to be more efficient and focused in how you gather your clients. Every time you get a project, identify the source that generated that job. Keep a list that you can refer to you during your brainstorming sessions. Since you've already set aside time to think about how to improve your business, you can wrap this in as well.

As with expense coding, look for patterns: Who are your good referral sources? Is there a common denominator between them? How can you find more like them? Think about how you can maximize those contacts and also about how you can thank them without fawning (you don't want to look pathetic and desperate).

Likewise, which referrals deliver high maintenance, low profit clients? Do the gorgeous ads you've placed all over town actually bring you any business? The startling truth is that very often the best leads come from just a few contacts.

In our friend Julia's case, after analyzing her referrals, she realized that her best clients and most profitable jobs all came from personal referrals from a parent at her son's school and that none came from her expensive magazine ad. What did she do? She decided to cultivate that contact, and to eliminate the ads.

CONCLUSION

So what's the bottom line here? Clearly there is lots to take in, but my own personal net-net would be to stop running all over town like a chicken with your head cut off. Just stop and think. Be quiet and analyze the data that is right under your nose. Take time to track, look at the results and make changes. Make it a lifelong habit. Open your eyes and start asking the right questions. Constantly seek out ways to improve. Make it fun. If you like to digest new bits of information by reading magazines, do that. Do you get inspired by blogs? Great! There is tons of information out there and there really is hope for your struggling business, you just have to stop and pay attention. Show it a little love, get to know it a little better, and tweak as you go. Everything—every relationship, business and project—is a work in progress. Keep searching for good answers and ways to improve, and implement your ideas along the way. If you try something and it doesn't work, stop doing it—faster than you would have in the past. You will be amazed at how much fun working on improving your business can be! And it all starts with that first step of diving in somewhere and trying to improve.

Part IV

LIFE AS A
SUCCESSFUL
ENTREPRENEUR

Chapter 14
THE TREES—TIME MANAGEMENT

OK, you say, now that job costing is a part of our company culture, what is my role exactly? Your new role, beyond what you *are* (speech therapist, designer of handbags, non-profit consultant, personal trainer, instrument repairperson, event planner, graphic artist, whatever!), is to *be* the entrepreneur. Essentially, you've got to switch from just doing your thing to actually working on your business. You must constantly be asking: How can I make more money? How can I improve my business? Where can I cut and become more efficient?

Expense coding provides the data from which you can answer these questions and then dream big, like you used to do before you got so bogged down with all of this garbage. But before you can dream big—think of it as viewing the forest—you've got to make the time to get a good look at the trees.

THE GLAMOROUS LIFE OF THE ENTREPRENEUR

In your new life as expert expense coding rock star CEO, trivial as these tasks may seem, you need to find the time to:

- Open every piece of mail. Yes, you, the big boss. I can't tell you how much easier it is to catch errors in billing, fraud, and God forbid, embezzlement when you have a strict mail policy in your office. (If you really hate this idea then have your assistant open all of the mail in front of you, separating out the junk and handing the real stuff over to you. Point is, no mail sneaks through the office without being scrutinized by your eagle eyes. You can open the mail two to three days a week, not necessarily every day, but you've got to open it. Period.)

- Approve job codes on all receipts and invoices before they are funneled to the bookkeeper. As you get more advanced, give your vendors the appropriate job code before they generate invoices, so that the bill comes to you with the job code already on it.

- Approve all invoices before they are processed for payment. Yes, *before*. It's too easy just to sign checks in a hurry, figuring you'll double back and check invoice accuracy later. You won't. Come up with your own system, but physically sign or initial every single invoice to be paid.

- Check timesheets for employees and independent contractors every day. Although doing this weekly might be easier, sorry. In the beginning, I want you to do it every day. Let's face it, if I say you can do it weekly, you won't do it at all. *Skim* through them, looking for problems—this shouldn't take you an hour (more like ten minutes—max).

- Check your bank balances daily. Don't panic! This is not as onerous as it sounds. All you're doing is a quick scan to make sure nothing is out of whack, which it usually isn't. And when something *is* out of whack, you'll be glad you caught it early. If you really don't have enough transactions to justify checking it daily, I'll cut you a little slack, but *no less* than two days a week.

- Review your job P&Ls weekly (even if a project or job isn't closed yet), studying the bottom line.

The majority of these tasks are about discipline. Since we are not sure exactly where the specific problems in your business lie, you must go through each of these steps in order to pinpoint the source of your troubles. Again, think of these processes as peeling back the layers of an onion. You're not sure which layer is rotten until you go piece by piece.

get boring. This is normal, par [...]
[...]n't mean that the process doesn't [...]
[...]eceptively simple. But in order to m[...]
[...]egularly make the time to power thro[...]
tasks.

Will the new process take some getting used to? Yes. Will it [...] *[...]solutely yes—I promise.* Just like when you first learned to walk, rite your name, or play the piano—it's hard. Your brain and your muscle [...]en't conditioned to perform in this new way. The synapses aren't firing ike they're supposed to, but they will! Stick with it, unfamiliar activities will become routine habits, and the results will blow your now peaceful, stress-free mind.

Dirty little secret time. Routinely, I find that I have to revisit these basics. I'm no different than any of you. I get busy, start a new division, am affected by the economy, make an occasional bad hire, lose my way and have to start again. When I get lost, stuck, turned around and discombobulated, these are the steps I return to. We all take our hands off the wheel once in awhile, but it's a matter of getting back in the car and facing forward. In fact, as I'm doing the final proof on this manuscript, I had a few little expense coding bubbles of my own to pop here at the office. Ironic, huh? It's OK, it really is part of the process. Determine your process, work it, tweak it, work it and then continue to adjust as necessary.

How to Squeeze All This In

Obviously, you will need to restructure your week so that there is time for expense coding. Time for the smaller, daily tasks like reviewing timesheets. Time for the weekly tasks of analyzing the project P&Ls, brainstorming and dreaming up ideas. And finally, time for the more long-term tasks of implementing those ideas. Remember, just like Michael Gerber says: Work on your business not in it. Work on your business not in it. Work on your business not in it. Repeat, repeat, repeat.

√ᴇᴇᴋ

...ryone works differently (we have morning people and n...
...inesses that are open 9-5 Monday-Friday, and businesses that
...the weekends), the common denominator we share is that we all
...actly the same amount of hours in a day and we all have to *build
...nto our schedules* to Code Your Way to Cash. You have to plan the
...k before you can work the plan.

Everyone's week is totally different, but because I'm often asked what my week looks like and how I plan for expense coding, I'm going to share it here. If you can extract something from my framework, steal at will! Here's what works for me.

First, Sunday is the day I plan my entire week. Being a working mother, this plan includes everything—from my Party Goddess! events to my speaking engagements to how to get my son to his doctor's appointment on Thursday.

Monday is the day I review all my reports, invoices, referral sources and so on. I see how many jobs we closed, and how many new clients we have coming in. Because I also do my coaching sessions on Monday, I have back-to-back appointments, but I always carve out time to review my scorecards to see what's happening in my business generally and what happened the previous week, specifically. (You don't have to choose Mondays, but pick one set day so everyone knows what to expect.)

By the time I leave on Mondays I'm exhausted, grimy and thrashed, but elated at the same time. I have a tremendous sense of accomplishment because I spent the day doing exactly what I should be doing, focusing on the numbers.

I pick another day of the week to be glued to my desk to handle the business aspects of running my company. I have two "out" days, where I cram in all of my appointments with new clients, vendors, site checks— anything that requires me to put on makeup and heels and drive. The fifth day is a floater where I insert all the miscellaneous stuff that needs to get done. It's also a day that I can be spontaneous—taking a client for an impromptu meeting or putzing around the bookstore looking inspiration for some new party theme I've got to create.

My plan for the week isn't set in stone. It can and does flex, depending on all kinds of things, some of them as simple as I'm tired and don't feel like planning the week on Sunday night. To compensate for that, I definitely get to the office extra early Monday morning to do the planning. If I haven't laid out the week by the time I take my first appointment or conference call on Monday, I'm toast.

I might adjust the plan for the week depending on how the previous week went. In fact, this just happened to me. Last week I had two days of back-to-back appointments, Monday and Tuesday. My Mondays, as you know, are always hectic, purposely packed full of scorecards, P&Ls, staff meetings, the works. But then Tuesday was the same way. I had coaching clients, party clients and meetings. Both of those jam-packed days took place at my office, which does *not* work for me. I'm a wanderer by nature. I love my office space, but I'm in sales and I do a lot of speaking engagements—I like to be out and about, having lunch, smiling and nodding, bringing in new business. For me, two days cooped up behind the desk is like a slow, painful death. I came home Tuesday night practically in tears—overwhelmed, frustrated and definitely *not* feeling very accomplished.

I asked myself, had I taken on too many clients? Or was this simply a case of too much of the same thing, two days in a row of back-to-back junk in the office? It turned out to be the latter. Because I was in touch with what works and doesn't, both for my organization and myself, I was able to root out the problem and schedule my next work week with more variety.

I also might adjust the plan depending on what I learn when I review the P&Ls on Monday. If I see, for example, that my staff all worked seventy hours last week and we didn't even have an event, I know something's up. Are we working on a big project or has this become a

ern? Is my team overwhelmed because we are understaffed for the
..ount of work we've got? Is someone underperforming? Or is it that we
..st started running a new ad and we're getting lots of calls? I assess the
situation and I adjust accordingly.

So, rather than just plan the work and work the plan, a more accurate
description would be plan the work, work the plan, adjust the plan and
work the revised plan.

YES, EVERY DAY

The first thing I do when I get to my office every day is to make a
list of the six most important things to do that day. And then I don't do
anything until I complete those Top Six tasks. Yes, it would be nice to
clean out my desk drawers, but it isn't essential and it doesn't make me
money. Some people like to make the list of tomorrow's Top Six before
they leave in the evening. When you actually make the list all depends on
how you like to work. What's important is that you have a list of the Top
Six most important tasks for the day. These are the things that, if nothing
else got done, keep us set and on track. We handle the biggest, most
important things before we tackle all the little stuff that sucks up our time
and leaves us with nothing to show for ourselves at the end of the day.
We certainly were busy, but we can't really say what we got done—story
of most of my life, by the way, so don't feel bad. By planning and doing
the Top Six, you didn't clean the drawer but you did have time to review
the monthly financial statements and course correct for next month—a
truly important task.

When you're new to expense coding, your Top Six is always going to
include *dealing with the money tasks*—the mail, the receipts, the invoices,
the timesheets, the bank balance. In the beginning, you will need about
thirty minutes per day to review all this information—thirty minutes that
you must *schedule* into your day.

Myself, I like to do the money tasks first thing, before I do anything
else and before anyone else even gets to the office. Why? I want to be

sharp and focused, so I can move through them quickly (afternoons, I'm slowing down and desperate for a double cappuccino).

And I shouldn't tell you this, but I will. There's hope—this won't always take thirty minutes. You will pick up speed. And, as you become more and more familiar with all the documents you are looking at, you might not have to do *every* task *every* day. Now that I've been job costing for more than ten years, I check my bank balance twice a week—I skim it, and I'm fast because I'm not sorting through an entire month's worth of transactions. I'm spot-checking, taking the temperature, getting a pulse. Hang in there, stick with those thirty minutes for a while, and then your time will come to mow and blow right through it.

TIME TO CODE YOUR WAY TO CASH (WHICH LEADS TO DREAMING)

Remember when we did our first expense coding case study back in Chapter 10, and I asked you to set aside a two-hour chunk of time? Well, you're going to need to *schedule a two-hour chunk of time every week* to do revenue and expense coding on a regular basis. This is a ballpark figure based on my experience. If you have a lot of back work, or your company is on the larger side, you may need more time per week until you get up to speed. If this is the case, I recommend you do several two-hour chunks of time rather than a marathon day that burns you out. We're going for sustainability here. You are going to have to stick with this for the rest of your business life. So, whether it's one two-hour chunk of time per week or five, *mark these into your calendar.* (As I said above, Monday is the day I do my expense coding and get my own personal State of the Union, so I know I'm on track for the week.)

During this two-hour chunk of time, you are not only reviewing your project P&Ls, but also generating lists of mini orange flags, with potential answers connected to the Big Three Questions. These are brainstorming sessions, and if you have to go into seclusion and be a hermit to get them, that's OK.

During these two-hour chunks of time, you will:

- Analyze your project P&Ls for all active projects to ensure that you're staying on budget. In addition, you will look at the P&Ls for any project that was completed the previous week. Look at the revenue and bottom line on each one. Do things look in order or grossly out of whack? (Example: Today I looked at a P&L for an active job because I wanted to see how many staff hours we had put into the event to date. On the detailed backup—the timesheets—for the P&L I noticed that one of my staff had put in nineteen hours on that project over the last couple of weeks. I looked at her figure related to everyone else's—which were much lower—and I realized the problem. The project is for a client who is also a vendor with whom this staff person works. The nineteen hours were coded to the *wrong* project. Had I not caught the error, it would have looked like the event for this client had gone drastically over budget, and it would have appeared that the amount of time we're spending with the vendor is less than it actually is. A simple mistake, caught because I review the project P&Ls weekly.

- Make a list of problems.(They might be huge Ahas! or just niggly little issues that you want to question or challenge.)

- Make a list of ideas for change. (These are your fabulous new ideas prompted by the Big Three Questions—how to raise prices, cut costs and become more efficient.)

- Figure out how much time the changes will take to implement.

- Prioritize the ideas.

- Delegate some of those ideas.

- Put the ideas into your calendar.

Most of the list above should look very familiar by now. What's new?— the last three bullet points. Don't worry, you're in the home stretch. These

tasks will help move you from *having* those great ideas to actuall[y]
them. And let's face it, that's where the fun begins.

WHEN TO IMPLEMENT THOSE GREAT IDEAS

Let's work on how to plan in the time for the big ideas. Go get you[r]
list of ideas for change from Chapter 12. Decide how much time that you
think it will take to accomplish each idea so you can determine which one
will give you the biggest bang for the buck.

For example, if one of your ideas to cut costs was to ask your rental
company to give you a 10% discount instead of a 5% discount on rentals,
how long would that activity take? Consider everything: The time to look
up the number, call, play a little phone tag, have the conversation, perhaps
even have a follow-up conversation. Don't cheat and guestimate that it
will take you two hours, really consider how much time it will take. Then,
add a little more time because we all tend to underestimate these things.
Do this for *every* idea you listed.

Now that you have a list of ideas *and the amount of time it will
take to implement them*, look at all your ideas and organize them into
these categories:

- High priority—activities that will give you the biggest bang for
  the buck because you'll spend the least amount of time and effort
  on them, and the financial rewards will be tremendous.

- Middle priority—Activities that will be helpful and save you some
  time and money for sure, but they probably won't rock your world.

- Low priority—activities that would be nice (we were brainstorming,
  after all, and any idea is fair game), but they are not likely to work.

Now, prioritize even further. Sort your high priority activities, putting
the single most important thing you can do immediately at the top. Next
would be something really, really important, and so on. Do the same
with your middle priority activities and your would-be-nice ideas. (If

nt to learn more about this kind of prioritizing, check out www.
inCovey.com.)

Finally, starting with high priority activities and working down the list
rough the would-be-nice ideas, decide when—a specific date—you will
have that activity completed. Be sure to consider how much time each
activity is going to take. I want you to be tough with yourself, but don't
say you're going to have every idea completed by next week because then
you'll end up in rehab. Be aggressive but realistic. Take your physical
calendar—whether you're using iCal, a Day-Timer, or a wall calendar—
and plug all those dates into the calendar.

Bravo! You have just created your game plan. Everything is now
broken down into specific, manageable action steps taking you from
where you currently are (stressed out and in trouble) to where you want to
be (wealthy and relaxed!).

At the end of each week, assess your progress and if necessary, transfer
any incomplete activities to the following week. You will revisit them
when you do your next expense coding session.

Are you feeling lean and mean in your new, disciplined work lifestyle?
You should! Pat yourself on the back, because *carving out the time to
focus on the numbers of your business is the most important thing you can
do as an entrepreneur.*

LET YOURSELF EAT CAKE

Congratulations on your new role as a big dog. Doesn't it feel good
to be in control and to be calm? (If you're not calm yet, right this second,
don't panic, it will come; you're probably still just in shock.) You have
the facts now, and are anticipating and planning ahead. Job costing
enables you to make decisions based on an accurate understanding of the
numbers. Job costing shows you where it's best to put your valuable time.
Job costing increases your profitability and improves your sense of self.

Because of job costing, you are living proactively, rather reactively—and your business is thriving. And when the business thriving, *you* are thriving and freed up to do what really makes yo heart sing.

Chapter 15
THE FOREST—DREAMING BIG

You're in the sweet spot—you've gotten rid of the silt and rocks and are left with the gold at the bottom of the pan. What's next? Where do you want to go with all this new information? What excites you? You can have some fun trying things, because you've done your expense coding homework. You've been collecting and analyzing the data, brainstorming about how to improve your business, and calendaring in the time to implement your ideas. *Regularly.* Now it's is time to dream really big, to step back and look at the forest, to set some overarching goals and add some color to this painting of yours. Get excited, the good stuff awaits!

THE WELL-PAID FISHERMAN

Think of yourself as captain and chief fisherman. Your job is to decide what waters to sail to and how you can reel more big fish into the boat in less time and with a smaller crew, all while taking a little time out to get a tan and drink a piña colada. Your job is not to fillet the fish, fry them, prepare the delish salsa that accompanies them, or even serve them. You get those fish in the boat, make sure they are halibut if you're fishing for halibut, and then you turn them over to your well-chosen first, second and third mates. Let your team handle the rest while you keep your eyes on the horizon.

Translation into business-speak: as the big boss, you should be focused on the overall company vision. Where do you want the company to go? What amount of sales and profit do you want to generate? What are the quickest, easiest ways to accomplish those goals? How can you improve the systems you have in place? Up until this point we've been scrubbing the decks. Clearing out all the old junk on that boat that didn't serve our vision. Take the facts that you've so carefully corralled and use them to create a much rosier and more liberating future. You know now what you did, what results you got, and most importantly what you can do to turn things around. Let's make some magic!

Connecting Profitability and Passion

Looking at your favorite projects, which *parts* of those projects were the most profitable? We can go back to my example of The Party Goddess! handling invitations for clients. When I looked at the invitation line item on our P&Ls and saw that invitations didn't turn a fabulous profit, I adjusted my advertising. I made sure it did not focus on doing big invitation pieces for events. I also saw that the décor line item regularly returned a high profit margin. Guess what? I love to handle décor. I love to design it, explain the theme to clients, shop for the components, surround myself with those beautiful items, and finally, execute my vision. I focused my marketing to find more clients that get jazzed by (and are willing to pay for) fabulous décor, which I knew was a high moneymaker for my company. A win-win!

Define Your Passion

Subjective, big-picture questions are important when you're talking about your passion. A successful business is based not only on what is most profitable, but also on what is most interesting and enjoyable to the owner. Remember Chapter 2? We've come full circle. Start with a clean stack of white paper and start dreaming in print—ask yourself:

- *What segments of my business do I enjoy most?* Designing business cards or creating websites?

- *How do I like to work?* From early in the morning to late at night in the office, or are you like me—do you need a little air under your wings a couple of days a week?

- *What inspires me?* Is it what used to inspire me? I started out handling social, corporate and non-profit events. Eventually I realized that while I loved to give to charity, I did not love to work on charitable events, so I let go of the majority of that kind of business. It's OK to change your mind. It's OK to evolve. In fact, those are good things and will help you get re-fired up about your business.

- *Who is the ideal client?* It might be different than who it started out to be. If you have different segments of your business, the ideal client might be different for each. Where does that ideal client live? I don't mean what's their address, although that could be part of it. I mean, where do their hobbies and their interests take them? What magazines do they read and where do their kids go to school? The Party Goddess! has defined our ideal client in great detail. I can spot that client a mile away because I know how old she is, what kind of car she drives, how many kids she has and whether her husband brings home the bacon or she does. I know her on paper and I know her in my gut. And, yes, I said "her." My ideal client is a "her" because she is more likely to be the emotional decision maker I'm after. The one who will see my website, fall in love, decide she just absolutely, positively, under any and all circumstances, must work with me, The Party Goddess! That's who I want. That raging, passionate client who wants a party of mine so badly she can taste it. Why? Because I know that when we're all done and the candles are blown out, she will become one of my raving fans. And raving fans bring me more business. And that's what we all need, as Kenneth Blanchard says, right?—1,000 Raving Fans.

- *Where do the opportunities lie?* In the midst of all of this dreaming about what you want to do, where you want to work, how long you want each day to be, and who you want to work with, ask yourself where the opportunities lie. A key aspect of running a successful business is looking for opportunities and striking while the iron is hot. Ask yourself (and your team) what kinds of questions your customers or potential customers are asking. It's like when you go to the grocery store and you ask if they carry a certain exotic spice and they say no because there isn't enough demand for it. Well, the smart supermarket knows that if five people in a week walk in and ask for the same exotic spice, there must be some demand—maybe everyone's watching the hot new cooking show on the Food Network. What are the demands, or market needs, that you could meet for your customers? Stop and think. Take a walk—yes, I'm serious. Just let the ideas flow. Take time to dream—it's where your most profitable ideas lie.

Break Out Your Magnifying Glass

At the end of the day, what is the point of job costing? Done start to finish, it let's you see the trees *and* the forest. To see one or the other, all you need to do is shift your focus. Tip your head up or down, depending on which part of the landscape you want to see. Do you need to do some work on the nitty gritty, or is the big picture dreaming what's necessary?

Your company may be well run but is in a bit of a mess or you wouldn't have bought this book. You've started cleaning house and casting light on the darker, more unknown aspects of your business. You've pulled apart some previous projects, broken them down by activity and type of expense, and seen where your time is *really* going. You have discovered your weaknesses—ouch. No, it wasn't much fun, but hauling boxes and disinfecting rarely is. Now that you've done all of the heavy lifting, though, whip out a magnifying glass and look at those project P&Ls and get ready to apply what we've learned to the future.

What jumps out at you? Which projects were the most profitable? If every time you worked with a developer, you had to work twice as hard for half the money and none of the praise, then maybe you don't want to work with developers in the future. Maybe every time you designed invitations for huge corporations you were thrilled because they paid on time, only needed you during regular business hours, and were so appreciative. So what do you do? Find more of those clients! Find your own personal intersection between your ideal client, profitability and passion. For me, that's the holy trinity of entrepreneurship.

In our gut, we all know which clients and which projects we want, but we often don't let that cat out of the bag. If we told anyone which clients we were specifically after, what would happen? Maybe we would turn away all of those other people who didn't fit the bill. Hopefully, yes, you would! Because business is based on economies of scale, and economies of scale are kind of like getting in the groove. Once you get in the groove, you can churn and burn a lot faster. If realtors are your target audience, and you start working with more and more of them, it gets easier because you're used to their schedule, lingo and ways of doing business. Ultimately, you can make more money.

Look at your book of past business and get an overview. Some of your projects might have been expense coded, or job costed, as part of your practice in reading this book, others haven't been, but that's OK. Just get an overview. Recall which were your favorite clients—projects that you could do all day long and not even notice the hours going by. *You want more of those clients.*

Case in point. Today I met with my newly hired salesperson. When she asked what kind of business I wanted her to get for The Party Goddess!, I didn't tell her to find just anyone with a credit card that would clear. I told her exactly who and what I was looking for: big social or corporate clients who place a high value on amazing décor. I didn't want 300 events this year that were all for $500. Rather, I wanted ten delicious clients that I could fall in love with. Because when I'm in love with my clients, I'm happy and I will work night and day for them. I will go the extra, extra mile. I will overlook the little things—maybe some of the vases come back chipped—because I like them. I give my business to people that I know like and trust me, and I look for the same kind of customers.

DRAW THE MAP

So what does your map look like? How many clients do you want to service this year and at what price point? How many surfboards do you want to sell and to whom? Based on everything we've dug up here on this journey, is it more profitable for you to sell single surfboards at a premium on the road to Hanalei Bay, or to sell tons of them at a much lower profit margin to one of the larger beach outlets?

A last bit of homework, for old time's sake. Before you wrap up this relationship of ours, I want you to dream a bit more, and flesh out the following on some—you got it—clean, white paper. Not in your head or to a friend, but right here, right now.

- *How many clients do you want to have in the next twelve months?* What do those clients look like and where do they shop, eat and vacation?

- *How many projects do you want to work on?* Lots of little ones, or a few big ones that will take the whole year?

- *Which parts of your business do you really want to focus on?* Coaching creative female business owners off the ledge, or helping single men in transition to their next career?

- *Where does your biggest challenge lie?* What keeps you up at night? What's the itch that you just can't scratch? I usually have three big challenges going at any one time, so don't feel bad if you've got more than one! Write them down in detail, spelling errors and all. By identifying your challenges and writing them down, you open the doorway for the solutions to come into your life. They are out there. Just keep looking.

- *Which areas of your business are you ready to put to bed?* Don't be afraid to call it a day. The sooner you do, the faster your energy will be freed up to focus on what you really want. Take this last one to heart. There are so many divisions and aspects of my business that I should have turned the lights out on a heck of a lot sooner than I did, but I didn't. Why? I hate to admit it, but my ego. I just didn't want to stand up and say that that idea wasn't the best and I'd be better off leaving it behind. Not fun, but definitely the right thing to do.

Your Maintenance Plan

Once you've fleshed out your goals for the year, you'll want to keep checking in with them at least once a month. Once a week is better. And once (or even twice!) a day is best. Do whatever you need to do to keep your goals and dreams in front of you. I write them down, cut out pictures that represent them, tuck reminders in my wallet, on my TV, by my bed and near my sink. Keep what you most want for your business, your customers and your life at the forefront of your consciousness. Lots of goal setting gurus believe that when you want to accomplish something you need to review your top goals every night just before you go to bed and every morning when you wake up. (If you want more on this subject, check out Jack Canfield's work. He's one of my absolute favorites, a true master at teaching how to accomplish what you dream about.)

When you need a little shot in the arm, go back to the basics. I already told you about my Top Six list for the day. Here's another of my superhero-come-to-the-rescue-right-now-because-I'm-fried tricks—my Top Five. Pick five things to do each week to improve your business, whether it's repainting the front door, upgrading your operating system or purging your files. Take a class on something you think might help get you recharged—whatever you do, keep learning, keep improving and keep stretching.

Stand Strong

Let me prepare you for something else. When you finish this book, you will probably feel elated, that there's hope, and that someone out there understands and "gets you." You are correct, I do understand, and I do "get you." All too well, believe me!

Don't let anyone or anything or any challenge or any struggle take the wind out of your sails. Naysayers are out there. Other business people or your banker or your lawyer or your spouse or your best friend will tell you that it's too much work to Code Your Way to Cash. What do you mean? You're going to start tracking all of your expenses and coming up with these codes? That's ridiculous. Who has time for that?

Who has time for that? You do. Choose to follow people who have been where you want to be. If your best friend is a million dollar business owner and she tells you this book and this plan is stupid, consider her advice (maybe). But if your friend is broke, burdened and out of sync with her own dreams, then cut her off at the pass. Be gracious but move on. You two can still be friends, but she doesn't need to be your business mentor.

Entrepreneurs who have built their businesses from the ground up and who are still passionate and learning to grow are the best ones to follow, for me anyway. Why? Because they have encountered and will continue to encounter the exact same things that you and I are dealing with on a daily basis. They know the whole entrepreneurial thing isn't all lollipops and rainbows.

So now it's time for me to bid you farewell. Now, it's time for you to dig in. Expense code. Job cost. Code Your Way to Cash. Your hands may come off the wheel. You may start daydreaming in your business, and before you know it, you'll have lost your way. That's OK. Start again. Pick yourself up, dust yourself off, keep trying. There's not a successful entrepreneur out there who doesn't have to refocus regularly. If they tell you that's not the case, they are either lying or you don't know them well enough.

Seriously.

HAVE MARLEY MAJCHER SPEAK AT YOUR NEXT EVENT OR ON YOUR NEXT PROGRAM!

Marley Majcher is available for keynote presentations and full-day seminars. She is a frequent guest and speaker at trade shows and conferences all over the globe!

Majcher knows that most speeches are pretty uneventful, to say the least. But why do they need to be? Marley uses her candid, edgy, motivational, witty, energetic and laugh-out-loud-funny style to make her points and engage the audience be it eight, eight hundred or two million television viewers around the world. Marley's boots on the ground, real world, totally practical tips on doubling your income, thriving as an entrepreneur and fattening up the bottom line by focusing on what really matters are the perfect antidote to another corporate or social snooze fest.

Marley's been featured on or in: Fox, Fox Business, E!, ABC, NBC, CBS, HGTV, *The Wall Street Journal, Chicago Tribune, Fortune, Los Angeles Times, BusinessWeek, Forbes, Entrepreneur, UsWeekly, People.* Her event client list includes Britney Spears, Pierce Brosnan, Katherine Heigl, Jennifer Love Hewitt, Snoop Dogg, Morgan Stanley, Shea Homes, See's Candy, Georgetown University, Art Center College of Design, Whole Foods and a ton more…

Visit www.MarleyMajcher.com for more information.

…But Wait, There's More!

NEED A LITTLE MORE PERSONAL ATTENTION TO CODE YOUR WAY TO CASH?!

Marley Majcher is available for one on one and group coaching for you or your organization. For years she has worked with individuals and corporations in a variety of fields from real estate and medical laboratories to graphic designers and makeup artists.

Majcher knows that a lot of the coaching programs out there don't "get" you and your organization or underestimate the amount of resistance that comes up to brand new ideas. Marley's years of experience with all kinds of personality types from brainiacs to off the charts creatives, ensures that she can reach your team members and effect the change to the bottom line you as the boss crave. Being an entrepreneur herself for so many years, she understands the inherent challenges and constant frustrations in running a business, feeling lost and overwhelmed amidst the sea of options. Marley's a pro at cutting through the baloney to get to the root of the problem and actually identify the real source bleeding the bottom line so you and your team can stop spinning your wheels and actually make some money!

So if you've had it being stressed out over what you thought was a boring topic, finance, you need to call Marley today. You can't imagine how much fun getting your act together and finally making the money you deserve can be.

Visit **www.ButAreYouMakingAnyMoney.com** for free weekly tips and tricks to fatten up your bottom line or for more information on a little coaching.